London, Flower of Cities All

A scene from Fanny by Gaslight. *(Endpapers)*

A baroque touch in Cutlers' Hall.

LONDON
Flower of Cities All

Text by RICHARD CHURCH
Drawings & Paintings by IMRE HOFBAUER

THE JOHN DAY COMPANY : NEW YORK

ACKNOWLEDGEMENTS

We would like to thank the following for lending drawings:

Argosy
Family Doctor
Financial Times
The Guardian
London Transport
The Observer
Post Office Savings Bank
La Voce

and Mr William Holden for his invaluable help and advice

© Richard Church and Imre Hofbauer, 1966

Library of Congress Catalogue Card Number: 66-24102

Printed in England

Lowe and Brydone (Printers) Limited, London

To
C.A.C
1898–1965
this book about
her birthplace

CHAPTER ONE

[1]

Guide-books to London appear seasonally, and almost as profusely as the foliage in her parks. This book is not of that useful but deciduous kind. It is a vagary, a conspiracy of impression between two friends.

One, the writer, is a native of London. His bones are sooty and instinctive with London. He has spent a long life trying to escape from her, just as a son, later or sooner, escapes from his mother. But in the escape is the guilt, and in the guilt is the renewal of the suckling love, the urge to closeness, the craving of the blood. That is why I write this little book, as a kind of expiation, an old man's completion of the circle, a return to where I began, London of the late nineteenth century, and so from there onward into the present day.

The other conspirator and bondsman knows London differently. He came to her from Middle Europe many years ago, for refuge. He found it, and he fell in love, as a foster-child does who has been rescued from horrors. But though he has remained in London, fastened by devotion, he sees her objectively; compares her possibly with other European cities as did the Scottish poet, that unfrocked Franciscan diplomat, William Dunbar. He too was not of her womb, but he too felt the pull, five hundred years ago, that Mr Hofbauer feels today, as they have looked at the annual procession between the Law Courts and the Guildhall.

7

Thy famous Mayor, by princely governance,
With sword of justice thee ruleth prudently.
No Lord of Paris, Venice, or Florence
In dignity or honour goeth to him nigh.

That sounds old-fashioned, and restricted, from a geographical point of view, but it remains true for the two characters who are trying to discover, and to isolate, the London who has mothered the one, and fostered the other. London has been, and is still disparaged by many people, in Britain and abroad, who cannot penetrate to the mystery which the rather hostile Wordsworth sensed as he stood one morning on Westminster Bridge, to exclaim

And all that mighty heart is lying still!

In that line is contained the secret of the two thousand years of London's history, and the myriad human stories which have contributed to that history. The articulation of a city may be compared with that of a forest, the trees for symbol of its institutions, the foliage for its people who flourish in their season, then fall to compost the future.

But this consideration does not differentiate London from any other great city. They all have their distinctive qualities; one might almost say personalities. 'Paris, Venice, or Florence' are immediately more distinguishable, more pronounced than London. All three are queens. I am still not sure what kind of a woman my mother London is. In some moods she is an old drab, whispering hoarsely to passing males at wet street corners, or from furtive doorways. Many poets and novelists have heard that voice. Indeed, for a few of them, this was the voice above the bedraggled slipper that absent-mindedly rocked their cradles, to a gin-sodden lullaby. So it seems from their books, in which they react to London with reproach and even savagery. I think of James Thomson's 'City of Dreadful Night'; of the novels of George Gissing, and the hundreds of London contacts in Dickens's tales.

Their London, hoarse, hungry and diseased, economically somewhat like the Calcutta of today, with a luxurious, teeming street-scene liable at any moment to explode into horror of poverty or other degradation, was the London into which I was born in the last decade of the nineteenth century. This was at the height of the splendour and riches of the British Empire. London was then the largest and wealthiest city in the world. Before I place myself in it as an individual 'spy' (the word used by Grub Street gossips in the seventeenth and eighteenth centuries), I will take a pigeon's-eye view of London, as though I were pointing it out to a visitor from abroad who knows nothing of her story, especially its tumid manifestation during the nineteenth century, with commerce over-reaching the aesthetic of a sanely proportioned civic life.

From the economic and political points of view the history of London in the nineteenth century, indeed of the whole of England, began toward the end of the previous century with the primitive introduction of machinery, and the outbreak of the French

The Lord Mayor's Show.

Revolution in 1789. Up to that time London was recognizably the same city as it had been, in social structure and habit, since the days when Chaucer's pilgrims set out from the Tabard Inn at Newington Butts on their way to the shrine of Thomas à Becket in Canterbury Cathedral. Even then, in the fourteenth century, the status of London as the political and commercial capital of the country was firmly pronounced, never again in British history to be changed. Not even the Fire of 1666, and the complete rebuilding of the central City, affected its commercial and political routine.

The geographical reason for this is obvious. The City of London lies at the head of the Thames estuary at more or less the first dry point and solid ground adjoining the banks of the river. This point is a natural pass from the south east to the interior of the country. Through it, invading marauders had to pass from the Continent, as did the later merchants. Though neolithic remains have been found, no mention of a settled city here was made by Julius Caesar in his *Commentaries*. It is still assumed that a recognizable urban growth did not take root until the time of the Emperor Claudius in A.D. 43, though there are persuasive theories that London was already a metropolis for Celtic Britain. Mr Michael Harrison presents this theory in his book *London Growing*.

This settlement followed the geographical necessity caused by the habits of the river at this place. The land on the south bank was swampy, and therefore building had to be confined to the north bank on the two firm clay hills which still elevate the buildings in the very heart of the City. Dominant over them is the cathedral of St Paul. Like that of Christchurch at Canterbury, it has had several incarnations. The original was built in the early years of the seventh century. This was destroyed by fire in 1087, and the second, of stone in Gothic aspiration, was begun at once. Enlargements and alterations were incessant through the devout centuries. The spire added in A.D. 1315 was 489 feet high, and might well be called an Exultation, the most lofty in Europe. A fire destroyed it in 1561, and there was no replacement. Religious passion had over-reached itself, and during the reaction the cathedral was used as much for secular as for religious purposes. It became a *bourse*, and the building was neglected by the chafferers who used it. No divine figure appeared on the steps of that temple to scourge them away.

Such was the pattern of London as it remained for nearly a thousand years. It was largely a city built of wood until the great fire in 1666 destroyed the nucleus and gave Caroline England an opportunity to rebuild on the ashes according to a plan, with wider streets and some degree of sanitary provision. This plan was offered by one of the greatest geniuses produced by England, Sir Christopher Wren. Mathematician, philosopher and administrator, he combined this intellectual equipment within the vision and sensibility of an artist. Had his plan been accepted in its entirety, the centre of the City round the new cathedral would have been as superb in structure as the Acropolis.

Two factors intervened. One was the nature of proprietorship as protected by existing land laws at that time. The other was the inveterate English crowd psychology which, even in the sparse population of England in the seventeenth century, was obstinate and determined in its pragmatism, its tendency to incoherent vagary when handling its communal structures. Dogged individualism already predominated in the decisions reached, especially in the local government of an already pronouncedly democratic community such as London had developed.

The usual English compromise was made with the genius in a minority. Christopher Wren's town planning was wrecked, but his cathedral was accepted. It rose on the ruins of the old Gothic building. Like its predecessor, Wren's cathedral dominated the City, giving it a Roman character not inappropriate to the increasing emphasis of its function in England, and indeed in Europe, as a mother of commerce.

Of the many semi-private churches built by merchants for their own worship adjoining their premises in the City, fifty were designed by Wren. He also planned several others outside the medieval walls of the City. His spires, turrets and towers have survived the wars of our own time, more or less intact, and their character is still prominent in the architectural personality of the oldest part of London. They are stylistic punctuations amid the concrete skyscrapers, and they stand conspicuous as perfectly modulated paragraphs by Dryden would be if imbedded in the columns of a twentieth-century popular newspaper.

After the Great Fire, legislation was passed to prevent the building of wooden dwellings and warehouses, so that London became a city of brick, modified in more recent times by stone and ferro-concrete. This last material, still a novelty, threatens to oust the other two, and to obliterate the individual character of London as she has presented herself hitherto. More and more nondescript cosmopolitan blocks of tall office buildings are either replacing or dwarfing the London known and loved in the past.

The interplay of a city's physical form with the articulation and growth of its people is a fascinating study which historians, architects, archaeologists and certainly novelists have not failed to pursue. The interplay offers a complicated puzzle to the student seeking to make a simplified picture of the growth of London through the centuries. One factor is clear, however. From the beginning of the pre-Norman eleventh century, the community of London began to show a certain characteristic and thereby to establish the evolutionary line which it was to develop decisively in the history of the nation. British democracy began in London. The people, few in those early times, were a mercantile agglomeration and therefore independent of the powerful feudal landlords who had parcelled out among themselves the rest of the country under the Norman kings. London was thus more or less free even of the Crown, and as its people's wealth grew by reason of their commerce abroad and their centralization of trade within the kingdom, they gradually pronounced their power, both financial and political, upon the scope of the Crown and the would-be depredations of the infamous baronry who were to play so avaricious a part in the control of the country other than in London. This was the general state of affairs in the relationship of London to the rest of the island as the centuries passed. It remains so today in spite of the enormous industrial growth in the Midlands and the North, and of the rivalry of the great towns, such as Birmingham, Manchester, Leeds and Bradford. London had rivals even earlier, but their opposition has dwindled, and no commercial competitors could prevent her from developing at a most alarming rate. By the early seventeenth century, the Scottish king James VI, when he came south to reign over Great Britain, exclaimed with dismay upon the monstrous growth of this great commercial centre. Two centuries later, Cobbett invented the title 'the Great Wen' for this ever-swelling tumour, which was still uncontrolled by any sense of town-planning or economic sanity.

Cobbett saw the effects of the beginning of the machine age as its infantile gestures coincided with the political releasements and upheavals of the French Revolution. He witnessed the capricious and violent changes of wealth as a consequence of the Napoleonic wars, and in particular that inevitable aftermath of war which seems always to result in an inflated economy whose falseness gives it a febrility that must result in a crash.

He saw English agriculture betrayed and ruined, and the resultant rush of country people seeking work in the new mills and factories which were being spored in the North, the Midlands and in London where the financial capital for such enterprise was mainly stored.

During the latter part of the eighteenth century the population of London was under three-quarters of a million. For a while, further expansion was halted by disease and bad housing. The City, still medieval with its narrow streets, dark and insanitary buildings, lack of water supply, of hospitals and open spaces, reacted like poison upon the country folk who flocked to the town. Their misery and poverty demanded some form of recompense. That recompense was gin. The death rate accordingly increased. The horrors of London life at that time are recorded in the cartoons of Hogarth and Rowlandson; later in the novels of Dickens and Wilkie Collins. To find similar conditions today one has to explore the streets of Calcutta and Bombay. Such enormous cities, like London at the beginning of the nineteenth century, have their historical beauty and their almost heart-rending graces and poetic auras, but the horror underlying these is something for which civilization is even yet to be called upon to answer.

The pause did not last. The growth of London multiplied after the Napoleonic wars and the emptiness of the South Bank took the overflow, in spite of the unhealthiness of the swampy grounds of Bermondsey, Lambeth and Battersea. Village after village outside medieval and Tudor London were swallowed up as bricks and mortar spread.

This absorption of village communities has given London a unique characteristic. Greater London today is like the chemist's molecule, consisting of many atoms. Those atoms—the villages which have disappeared into the vast corporation—survive as ghosts to haunt the big road junctions within the town where suburbia allows old provincial houses, churches, inns and town halls to be seen cheek by jowl with the structures of the Victorian industrialist and Edwardian jerry-builder. Even nearer to the centre, such nuclei as Shepherd Market, Marylebone High Street, Paddington

Church Row, Hampstead.

Green, Highbury, Camden Town and Notting Hill Gate, have contrived to keep a village closeness, almost a secrecy within the urban landscape.

The small shopkeeper is to be found there, serving the sodality of near neighbours who are ready to help each other, to gossip, to scandalize and finally to rally against any threat to their miniature corporation. These communities are comparable to village folk in their static way of life. When I was a boy in Dulwich in the first decade of the twentieth century I had many schoolfellows who had never been over Denmark Hill in London. Yet we were only four miles from Charing Cross. In the previous century such a belated, vestigial social structure served in some degree to maintain a corporate virtue and coherence in a London that otherwise would have been infinitely more shapeless. It is probable that the moral and religious affiliations by which London has hitherto saved itself as a community with a soul, were first articulated in these sub-centres obstinately resolute not to be annihilated in the general levelling and standardization toward which all urban growth tends.

13

At the beginning of the nineteenth century London was still predominantly sited on the north bank of the Thames between the forest of Epping on the east, the heights of Hampstead and Highgate on the north, and the pleasant meadows of Middlesex on the west. Westminster was still distinct from the body of the town, and Chelsea was a separate village. John Constable made several water colour sketches and drawings of the wild country of Hampstead Heath, from whose heights the Thames Valley could be surveyed with London lying as a wholly visible entity due south.

The poet John Keats, a cockney born in Islington, spent the last two years of his short life in a house on the edge of Hampstead Heath, and his near neighbour on the adjacent Highgate Hill was Coleridge. Keats's description of his walks on the Heath and his occasional longer journeys on foot down to Guy's Hospital in the Borough, where he was a student, are full of the fragrance of the countryside rather than of the smoke and fog which subsequently became the dominant feature that was to colour the literature of the period, notably the novels of Dickens and the poetry of Thomas Hood.

South of the river the encroachment had begun, but villages hardly more than four miles from London Bridge or Charing Cross, such as Dulwich, Clapham, Wandsworth and Lewisham were still rural, with their structure confined to the High Street and its miniature municipality.

Changes became more rapid under the impulse of the wealth pouring into the country from India and the growing colonies of the British Empire. Wealth was also exfoliating within the country, especially the North. As fortunes grew the more prosperous industrialists established themselves in and around London. This created a further growth westward of expansive suburbs: Belgravia, Pimlico, Holland Park. Few of the newly-rich arrivals wanted to live east of London because of the fog and smoke that swept over it before the prevailing south-west wind. Further, dockland lay below London Bridge and grew concurrently with the demands of the commercial world. The Isle of Dogs was the nucleus of the expanding district of wharves and docks which spread along both shores of the Thames estuary, gradually reaching as far as Gravesend in Kent and Tilbury in Essex. These sinister quarters attracted a cosmopolitan population and the extremes of vice, crime, and the picturesque heroisms which always accompany the more violent activities of mankind.

Dockland became a world unto itself as the labyrinth of lanes and wharves grew into an inconsequential mass of land and water, iron and brick. It has appealed to the historians of crime and the novelists who are fascinated by human drama in its more sordid and bestial manifestations. Thomas Burke and H. M. Tomlinson are notable recorders of this scene. Tomlinson's prose draped the scene in a sombre beauty.

The squalor and filth of that dockland beyond the east end of London can be imagined only by a melodramatic effort of mind. Labour for man-handling the car-

Carlisle Mansions, Victoria.

goes was casual and recruited from unorganized mobs who alternately starved and caroused. The men's conditions of labour and economic status were not to be changed until the end of the century, when the Liberal politician John Burns, and the Union leaders Ben Tillet and Ernest Bevin fought for better conditions and a gradual organization of the dock labourers.

At the opposite extreme, the people profiting from the increasing wealth of the City, much of it through dockland, were settling in the pleasant uplands that formed the rim of the London basin. Highgate, Hampstead and Harrow to the north; Dulwich, Norwood, Sydenham and Blackheath to the south, changed from country villages to exclusive suburbs studded with large villas and parklike gardens established by merchants, bankers, stockbrokers and lawyers, who were driven to Town daily in their horse carriages.

Some of the bankers were settlers from abroad. On Denmark Hill, for example, a magnificent villa was built by a German, who there entertained Mendelssohn. It was in the garden on Denmark Hill that the now hackneyed 'Spring Song without Words', was composed. When Richard Wagner came to England he stayed in the same house. A little further toward the crest of the hill John Ruskin, son of a rich wine merchant, was born in 1819. He was to develop into the eccentric critic of the terrifying new economy of industrialized Europe, and to utter his jeremiads against the influence of the machine as it was debauching the handicrafts which since the beginning of time had determined the shape and texture of human manufactures.

The new processes designed and carried out in the factories imitated and replaced those of the yard and the workshop with disastrous results. Natural, traditional taste and the classical sense of proportion emerging from the mystique of the Golden Number were overlaid by the clumsiness of these first products of the machine-made process, and the still experimental methods of mass production. Further, the possibilities of quick fortunes and larger profits played a part in the degeneration of the whole aesthetic of communal life. Homes had to be provided cheaply and quickly for the ever-increasing numbers of workpeople drawn into this expansion. Speculators and adventurers, with their shoddy methods, dominated the growth.

The results of their efforts survived almost intact until the second world war. Suburb after suburb spored in an appalling uniformity of petty dwellings in the back streets where were housed the clerks, the shop-assistants and other servants of the new monster bred by machine. These conditions shaped the growth of London at that time. The swamps on the south side of the Thames were filled in. Battersea and Bermondsey no longer harboured waterfowl. Leather and soap factories, breweries and a myriad of private workshops arose amid a confusion of side streets peopled by diluted humanity in which the original London-born cockney was often a minority.

There is a boat at the end of the street. King George V Docks.

It must not be imagined, however, that these people were degraded into a faceless and unified industrial population. They suffered from an unstable economy and dread of unemployment, but they were still individuals unconditioned by highly organized newspaper propaganda, by compulsory schooling and other such levelling influences as condition our social life in the second half of the twentieth century. Big business had not yet consolidated to make these town dwellers eat, drink and clothe themselves according to the dictates of a few master organizers at the top. Right up to the first world war, within the recollection of people still alive today, the variety and idiosyncrasy of personal appearance, dress, dialect, standards of education, religious principles, hobbies and other aspects of culture, still marked the differences, from one family to another, in these monotonous little back streets.

I can recall a street in Battersea, in the 1890s, where a Scotsman from Aberdeen earned his living as a lift-maker. He worked for himself as a contractor handling the cabinet work of those early lifts, which were then of an elaborate rococo architecture. His two sons later worked with him, though when I knew them they were still boys at an elementary school. One of them took to making violins, and his instruments found considerable reputation both at home and abroad. Further along the street lived a man who was a commissionaire, who marched away smartly every morning, left-right, left-right, almost preening himself in his uniform, with its buttons and patent leather straps. He too was a Scotsman, brother of a professional soldier who had risen from the ranks to become a general who won distinction in the Boer War—one Hector-Macdonald. His next-door neighbour was a postman, who achieved a local fame as a grower of chrysanthemums of gigantic size and superb coiffure in a small greenhouse built in the yard behind his semi-detached villa. Opposite him lived a quaint old couple of benevolent reputation. Everybody loved them. The husband owned a four-wheeler horse cab (called a 'growler') which he drove himself from morn to night somewhere in the mysterious West End of London. It gave him a comfortable living; so much so that his old wife, who might have passed as an embodiment of David Copperfield's Aunt Betsey Trotwood, was a fairy godmother to all the children who played in the street. She dispensed chocolates and sweets liberally to those urchins, many of whom were bare-foot and half-starved.

The need for playgrounds and other open spaces had not been considered when the lay-out of these suburban settlements was determined. As neighbourhoods degenerated and the more successful inhabitants moved outward to newer suburbs, the less provident and less hard-working outcasts from the merciless economy crowded closer into the decaying inner suburbs. The children of these slums had no open-air life other than that found in the gutter.

When the nineteenth century dawned the whole of England contained hardly more than ten million people. Today Greater London includes over eight million. The

The mendicant.

18

cancerous growth of urban populations, even on the smaller scale within that ten-million population, alarmed the Government, and a Municipal Reform Act was passed in 1835. Still more important toward the improvement of the quality of urban life was the passing of the Education Act in 1870 by Mr Gladstone. Elementary education became compulsory. This laid the foundation of the modern scene, for from it sprang the popular press, with all its faults and its virtues, and the nationwide pseudo-literacy of the population. The benefits of this process are obvious, though much of the idiosyncrasy of individual life tended to be ironed out under the increasing efficiency and organization of the educational and journalistic machines, which were to make social life smoother and consequently flatter. This was reflected in the London scene, though not so markedly as today. It changed the habits of Londoners as Dickens and Thackeray had portrayed them. It began the osmotic pressure of one class into another, and the trend toward equality.

As these changes gathered pace, the insular homogeneity of the London scene began to be undermined. The coming of the Prince Consort to England had already begun the process. His influence upon the relationship of the Queen with her Ministers and Parliament, though unpopular at first, was in the direction of a constitutional, even a Fabian development, in harmony with the historical gestures being made by the industrial growth of the nation and the necessary bias toward a democratic and bureaucratic control. This made for a more coherent organization of local government under the responsibility of the State. Prince Albert worked as a devoted servant, and killed himself in the effort. He promoted the Great Exhibition of 1851, housed in Hyde Park under a gigantic glass-house called the Crystal Palace, designed by the Duke of Devonshire's head gardener, Joseph Paxton. The Exhibition brought persons and products from all parts of the world to be shown in London, to be marvelled at, and to be absorbed into our hitherto parochial, insular way of life.

From that single enterprise, an acceleration of the return of London cultural life to the comity of Europe may be dated. The immediate result may have been incoherent and lacking in a sense of proportion, but it began the drift of a larger provision of contacts abroad which might enrich the manners and life of London. Perhaps Thackeray, rather than Dickens, was the spokesman of this development. He was born in India, and could see from outside the significance of this process of absorption which was making London something more than the capital city of the British people.

With the growth of the upper-middle-class suburbs westward, an army of domestic servants was employed in maintaining and running the extravagant family houses, with their mews filled with highly-bred horses, and their broughams and landaus. In addition there appeared fleets of four-wheelers and hansom cabs which could be summoned by a shrill whistle blown by a footman or other call-boy. For more general transport there appeared the omnibus pulled by two horses, and in the latter decades of the century the omnibuses were augmented by horse-drawn trams whose gay colours, pink, blue, yellow, brown, indicated the districts which they served. The

Highgate Village.

predominant noise of London throughout the century was the clatter of hooves on granite setts with which the road was paved.

The smell of horse-droppings gave a countrified tang to the atmosphere of town, and there was no lack of manure for the back gardens of the thousands of villas. Crossing sweepers and road scavengers augmented their wages by removing and peddling the manure. Horses pulled the tradesmen's vans and the heavy drays that came up from the docks to the warehouses. The fire-engine, postal van and milk churn were horse-drawn. The milkman's chariot (similar in form to that of a Roman centurion) went on its morning round hung about with dozens of oval pewter cans which he filled from a large churn in the body of the chariot and deposited at customers' front doors. Dust, flies and disease were ignored. Pasteurization was still not practised. Bovine tuberculosis was common amongst children. Disease and high mortality were incidental among the wealthy and middle class children as well as among the great majority of the under-nourished. Dickens's picture of the death of 'Little Nell' represented the fate of so many infants during the nineteenth century in London. Primitive remedies were still applied. I was one of the victims of bovine tuberculosis, and I was sent to a sanatorium on the Kent coast, where the 'cure' for this indisposition was a supervised dose of mustard with my meals.

The second special influence in changing the face of London was the building of the great railway termini and the streets of dwellings round them for housing the railway workers. These depressing areas survive today in such districts as Kings Cross, Euston and Waterloo. The only termini that made any concession to an architectural standard were the pseudo-Gothic St Pancras Station built by the Midland Railway, and Euston built by the London and North Western Railway. No effort, in the competitive gamble, was made to economize on the space, the siting, and on the harmonization of the railway buildings and tracks with the city as a whole. The heart of the town was ringed with these huge and hideous stations from which smoke and sulphurous fumes polluted the air, adding to the Dickensian fogs and the resultant respiratory diseases characteristic of Victorian life in the industrial towns, and particularly in London. These railway heads, with their sidings and shunting yards, occupied more than three hundred acres of valuable land in the heart of London. That is an economic anomaly yet to be disposed of.

I look back on that scene, London at the turn of the century, and see it as one of darkness and danger, hovering at the threshold of my home. Historians and sociologists record, and I can agree with them from my own experience, that the century came to an end with family life still the stable element in the social scene, and the feminine influence still active from the home rather than from an abstract maternal authority in Parliament, and municipal government.

Though it may seem contradictory to present the London of the nineteenth century as an individual mother figure, and then to qualify this by showing the various layers that comprised the scene and the community, nevertheless there remains a kind of historical eidolon, as a hovering figure, real if not tangible, which we may call the mature and august London as she reigned supreme in the nineteenth century. We know in fact that there have always been a hundred different Londons, each secreted somewhere within the community and only to be found by those spirits congenial to it. The London that Chopin saw was not the same as that which the poet Heine found. The French wine merchant visiting Mr Ruskin senior on Denmark Hill met yet another London from that cultivated by Henry James, the American novelist. The majority of Londoners were restricted by circumstances and small economic opportunity to the circle within which they were placed.

That was the London which mothered me, and as a present impressionist I am likely to offer a picture whose light, shade and overtone are determined by those surviving tinctures that not even the violent stirrings of the war-maddened twentieth century can dispel.

Charing Cross Station. The last Eleanor Cross.

CHAPTER TWO

[1]

That image of the violent stirrings of the twentieth century at once brings to mind the form of a spiral. It is a universal form which appears in the growth and the articulation of all things, from the spirochaete, (named after it), to the star-clusters. We can plot the organism of our individual lives that way, beginning with our birth at the base point, from which we move upward and outward in widening whorls of experience, to end—but probably, if the graph be followed, not to end; to go on, ever widening, into the unknown.

To look at London in the same way is profitable, for it provides the necessary increase of range, and at the end no determination, therefore no end. For London goes on also, thereby maintaining her own mystique, within twin periods of time and space whose climax no individual is equipped to foresee.

I begin upon the pivot of Charing Cross, the most widely recognized signpost, though not historically the earliest. And to try to counter the burden of the past, I shall move anti-clockwise, thus ensuring that I go in harmony with my companion who by the needs of his medium as a painter, must see London as she is, not as she was.

It is within this close confinement of streets, on a radius of half a mile from Charing Cross, that the Londoner feels most at home. If he is away from it nostalgia sets him gasping like a fish out of water. Though of my own choice I have lived isolated in the country for over a quarter of a century, I still take a snuff of the grimy air when I step

The bend of the River at Blackfriars. (Overleaf)

24

out of the train at Charing Cross Station, and I make a little mumbling murmur to myself, like an infant grunting with satisfaction at its mother's nipple.

Dickens wrote to his friend Forster from Switzerland, where he had gone to seek a quiet session at the writing of *Dombey and Son*. He said:
'... the difficulty of going at what I call a rapid rate is prodigious. I suppose this is partly the effect of the absence of streets. I can't express how much I want these. It seems as if they supplied something to my brain, which it cannot bear, when busy, to lose. For a week or a fortnight I can write prodigiously in a retired place; and a day in London sets me up again and starts me. But the toil and labour of writing, day after day, without that *magic lantern* is immense.'

As the train crawls between London Bridge Station and Charing Cross, a panorama of post-war London, a lanky rectagonal phoenix, lies in depth. The new multi-storeyed buildings flatten the old. Big Ben and the further westward minaret of the Roman Catholic Cathedral at Westminster, that formerly soared above the town, now appear to be withered, like frost-stricken ferns. Once upon a time the River façade between Charing Cross and Blackfriars Bridges was a dominant feature of Central London. It could be distinguished from as far as the Crystal Palace Parade on Sydenham Hill, six miles away; a placid white line half sunk in the near and central foreground, the former of suburban woodland and roofs, the latter of roofs, spires, chimneys, and skeins of smoke. I could distinguish the horizontal of Somerset House, and the two tall masses of the Savoy and the Hotel Cecil hovering in the air, their anchorage lost in the confusions of distance.

It was a fairylike scene, whose quality was retained, but with more emphasis, in the close-up view from the train drawing into the approach to Charing Cross from the South Bank.

But those proportions, familiar to me, and majestic enough, at the turn of the century, are changed today. A note of arrogance, a Babylonian emphasis, commands that same scene, to make it shorter but more forceful. The Hotel Cecil, to the west of the Savoy, was the biggest in Europe. Only its northern façade on The Strand remains. The main block on the river, behind the Victoria Embankment and Gardens, was rebuilt as Shell-Mex House in 1931, with a central tower whose clock is larger than that of Big Ben.

Looking north and westward, we see other dwarfings by new concrete, the Vickers skyscraper towering from beyond Lambeth Bridge and reducing the stature of the Houses of Parliament: the Hilton Hotel further in, but no less conspicuous; the still more flagrant intrusion at the other end of Victoria Street, near the Station, whose *lèse-majesté* destroys the privacy of Buckingham Palace. But privacy is of small significance in a democracy. It is thought to savour of privilege, of hierarchic mysticism, the veiling of the gods from the common gaze. These are attributes of the past, and have no place in a world opened up under glass buildings and the accuracies of the computer.

The new features, every one of which tends toward the destruction of London's unique personality, may be seen as a whole from the top of one of them, the new Shell Building on the South Bank, between Waterloo Station and the River. Looking north, our view is unbroken to the hills of Highgate, Hampstead and Harrow. On a bright midday they stand up, sun-drenched, with tiny church-spires ascendant. They seem to be watching the great, tumbled mass of human artifacture spread over the plain. No matter how conservative one may be, the novelty of the white shafts of post-war tower blocks cannot be offensive. They punctuate the rhythm of the older roofs, and give a defiant gesture to the ancient passivity of the scene: a Sienese touch, though these towers are commercial, not the pride-symbols of medieval power-mongers.

They mark the view southward also, and with the same dynamic effect. Over Bermondsey, to the east, a galaxy of them rises out of what used to be slumland. These are blocks of flats, the white cliff-sides broken with coloured patches of washing hung out to dry on the little balconies, scale upon scale. Round their bases smoke lingers, caught perhaps in a down-draught from those perpendiculars. It comes from the chimney pots, still in their myriads, from the streets of Victorian dwellings that survived the air-raids of the 1940s. Bermondsey Parish Church remains also, to mark what was once a village with its green. The scene is peaceful now, the only movement that of the cranes, like giant praying mantises, on the wharves along the waterside. They will have to pray harder if London Port is to maintain its place in world commerce.

Turning sunward from Bermondsey, away from the distant prospect of Shooters Hill and the sharp rise of Greenwich Park and Blackheath nearer to Town, we see more of this confining upland, the rim of the saucer into which London was first spilled. She is over-filling it today, and Forest Hill, Sydenham Hill, Champion Hill, Herne Hill, Denmark Hill (now we are looking due south) stand up, somewhat shadowed under the midday sun which glares behind them. All are covered by the overspill, which runs in rising roads, and parallel roof-lines, up and over the crests. Here and there are green patches, notably the large oasis of Dulwich with the brick tower of St Dunstan's Church on Red Post Hill, at the approach to Dulwich Village main street, that runs southward, up to Sydenham Hill and Crystal Palace Parade, where as a boy I used to stand spell-bound by the prospect of my native City, of which I knew so little, but dreamed so much.

Further removed, and widening out with less definition, over the Battersea levels, the landscape rises to distant Wimbledon, past Clapham and Wandsworth, crowded suburbs now but still to be distinguished by their Commons. North Side, Clapham Common, was the centre during the early nineteenth century of the Evangelical Sect of which William Wilberforce and Lord Macaulay's father were founder members. To balance any austerity that might be lingering in those gloomy mansions, Graham Greene, Roman Catholic apologist and novelist, lived there a century later.

Westward, looking up the Thames valley, there is little to be selected: a monotone of roofs, church spires, small factories, shabby schools, and one or two cemeteries like close clusters of mushrooms. The weather plays over this expanse, coming up from the western counties. Sometimes a smoky sunset spills a momentary beauty over it, before the street lights and neon signs take over. It is a sombre picture, ominous in its vagueness.

London Bridge seen from Hay's Wharf.

There is nothing to recommend Hungerford Bridge, which carries the railway into Charing Cross Station. Its hollow iron tubes take up the rumbling of the trains and multiply it until it becomes an earthquake. The deep subterranean din reverberates along the Victorian Embankment, and grumbles in the foundations of the Adelphi, whose crypt-like tunnels, built by the Adam brothers in the eighteenth century, still show a masterly brickwork that supported the terrace and a superstructure once the most graceful piece of architecture in London. It was replaced in 1936 by a gloomy pseudo-Babylonian pile that bullies the whole neighbourhood. The influence of its barbaric personality is even more depressing than the minute-gun earthquakes from the Hungerford Bridge.

I have always marvelled at the powers of endurance possessed by Bernard Shaw who lived for many years at No. 10 Adelphi Terrace, at the western end near the bridge. Opposite, at the river end of the block standing at a right-angle to the Terrace, lived J. M. Barrie, still nearer to the din. At the eastern end of the Adam Terrace the bohemian Savage Club was housed. Dominating even the hubbub of bonhomie there, this periodic cannonade from the Bridge recurred to send a shudder over the surface of the liquid refreshment in glass or cup. When the Festival Hall was built, a considerable part of its cost was due to the need to eliminate the percussive music from the Bridge. The concert chamber had to be sealed within the fabric of the building, like an egg within the egg-cup.

How much simpler the town-planning problems of twentieth-century London would be if the railway terminus had been set at Waterloo, alongside that of the line from Wessex. A small station already stands there, and at the time the two were built, the surrounding area was open ground. It became a slum without ever having been a respectable quarter of the South Bank. The terraces of workmen's dwellings built by the railway companies rapidly degenerated. Lambeth Cut was notorious at the turn of the century. Even so, the music-lover could go at that time to Miss Bayliss's Old Vic Theatre, to sit, at the cost of sixpence, on a bench and enjoy the opera so vigorously presented there. The poet W. H. Davies lodged in a doss-house there, called The Farm, after he gave up the profession of hobo in America and mendicant in England. The publisher-novelist Michael Sadleir paints a lurid picture of the streets around Waterloo Station a century ago, in his novel *Fanny by Gaslight*.

A modern railway terminus in the continental manner, such as that in Milan, could be built behind the Festival Hall and the huge commercial blocks that gather toward the new Waterloo Bridge, that graceful monument to Lord Morrison of Lambeth, the policeman's brat from Brixton who, with the East End timber merchant George Lansbury, devoted his life and passion to the betterment of working-class London. They were two great cockneys, and they will not be forgotten.

I have sonorous recollections of the replacing of Rennie's Waterloo Bridge by the present one in the 1930s, for I was living at that time in chambers in Lincolns Inn. Day after day, for year after year, I worked in my study beside Inigo Jones's chapel, to the distant but pervasive *basso ostinato* of pile-drivers from the river. With each thud, the little gouts of sunshine, or follicles of fog (according to the season) over my table gave a little squeeze, as though by contagion, the pressure communicating itself from the bed of the river through the sub-soil below the Strand, the Temple Gardens, and Chancery Lane, to give a miniature jerk to my fountain-pen, and an interjection to my train of thought.

Every afternoon I went down with my Aberdeen terrier to the Victoria Embankment, to see the work in progress. The strange thing is that the thuds at close quarters were less percussive in effect upon my ear than when they bludgeoned me during my morning's work.

I was not sweet-tempered about the perennial interruption for I mourned the disappearance of Rennie's exquisitely proportioned bridge. But conservatism of taste is sometimes no more than inertia, a force that works both ways in the physics of civilization. The new Waterloo Bridge, Morrison's pride, and the architect Gilbert Scott's achievement, proves to be as graceful in its rhythmic spans as its predecessor. What ugly company it has to keep round the curve of the river to Charing Cross; the all too vocative Hungerford Bridge that carries the trains so unnecessarily into the railway

The York Watergate

33

station which fills an aesthetically strategic position in the heart of London, and prevents any imaginative improvement on a site over which Nelson, on his nearby column, is fortunate in being able to turn his blind eye!

Even today, however, the little enclave of streets east of Charing Cross Station still known as The Adelphi, is a pocket of history that keeps the Palladian quality established by the brothers Adam in the eighteenth century. What they gave was additional to earlier survivals, from the Durham House, formerly on the site, one of the ducal palaces that faced the river. The building of the Victoria Embankment from Blackfriars to Westminster Bridges by Bazalgette in 1864–70 covered what remained of the gardens of those great mansions. So too disappeared the site of the blacking factory where for a few months Charles Dickens was employed as a boy by his cousin who owned it. The experience produced an attack of self-pity which left a permanent scar on the character of that volatile and over-sensitive genius.

There is still a terrace walk along the Adelphi front, but it is a sad substitute, frowned over by the brick block where once the forty-one windows of the Adam terrace smiled in welcome to the reflected sun-glare from the river, warm and confiding.

The Embankment is a monument to the triumph of iron, which in the nineteenth century began to intrude upon the function of timber and stone, much to John Ruskin's disgust. The lamp standards with their dolphins, and the seats with their sphinxes and camels, record this brittle intrusion, and also the theme of Empire so exciting to the Victorian community. From time to time new memorials are added to the Embankment, a practice begun in 1877 when Cleopatra's Needle was brought from Egypt, and after shipwreck on the voyage, set up on a projection into the river. The Royal Air Force Memorial was set in a similar position after the first World War.

The only relic of the great houses is the York Watergate from that built by the Duke of Buckingham in the seventeenth century. It faces York Buildings by the Embankment Gardens, which have removed it from the waterside. It takes its name, and its origin, from an earlier palace on the site, once the London seat of the Archbishop of York.

The most pleasing entry to this handful of streets that drop from John Adam Street, which is the northern boundary of the Adelphi, is through a gateway between the Gardens and a winedive (notable for its sherry drawn from the cask) at the bottom of Villiers Street that runs down from the Strand beside the brick arches of the railway station. These draughty arches were once a dormitory for the down-and-outs. Villiers Street has always been raffish, and is appropriately named after King Charles II's evil genius, Buckingham. It specializes in sleazy cafés and those pseudo-chemist shops which openly display aphrodisiacs, contraceptives, and paper-covered books about flagellation.

Wild life in the Parks.

Fairyland from the bridge of St James's Park. (Overleaf)

34

The gate opens on a footpath, which passes the York Watergate, and gives access to Robert Street and Buckingham Street, where some houses built by the Adam brothers survive. *The Fortnightly Review*, founded in 1865 by Anthony Trollope, was a monument amid the London literary scene during the second half of the nineteenth century and the first half of the twentieth. It had its office latterly at the bottom of Buckingham Street, up a panelled staircase, in panelled rooms. The contributor going to visit the Editor was almost bemused into producing a snuff box, and flicking the grains off his lace cuffs with a cambric handkerchief.

Further up, and still on the western side of Buckingham Street, Nos. 10 and 12 also have literary associations, in the appropriate setting of low ceilings and panelled walls. This row of what were once private houses was built in 1670, four years after the Great Fire. Samuel Pepys lived for a while at No. 12, and later in the end house overlooking the river. His nights and days were not disturbed by the simulated earthquakes which possibly helped to make Bernard Shaw so nervous a critic of his contemporary scene. Pepys heard only the night-watchman, with lantern and staff, and the street vendors by day. That daytime traffic survived long after the night-watchmen were replaced by a police force and street lamps. The muffin man, the knife-grinder, chair-mender, lavender-seller were still to be heard, each with a singular cry to draw attention to his trade, right through the years until the end of the first decade of the twentieth century. Old Londoners today can remember the song of the shawled women up from the lavender fields of Mitcham (also famous for its watercress beds), carrying a few sprigs in hand, above the large basket, and walking slowly down the middle of the road.

The muffin man appeared on Sunday afternoons. He moved like a mobile caryatid, balancing on his head a long, narrow tray covered by green baize. Beneath the baize a long white napkin protected the crumpets. He had a neat gesture as he swung the tray down from aloft, to reveal the padded crown on which the burden was balanced. The handbell with which he augmented his advertisement through the streets was set down on the ground while he dealt with his customers at their front doors.

The knife-grinder and chair-mender made slower progress, for their successful contacts meant longer stops over each job. The grinder twirled his stone by foot-treadle, in a two-wheeled contraption which he pushed by hand. Or if he was in a bigger way of business he had the machinery mounted on a float with donkey or pony in the shafts. Sparks flew from the contact of the wheel and the un-stainless steel of the household cutlery.

The chair-mender usually had a touch of the gypsy in his manner and person, and this made housewives wary. He usually carried an old chair-frame as trademark, and long coils of straw, rushes, and thin cane worn as a bandolier. He squatted tailor-fashion on the doorstep to re-seat the chair brought out by his customer, a job done so dexterously that it served to counter his sinister appearance, a foreign-ness intimidating to suburban eyes. But like the seasonal onion-sellers from Brittany, he brought a touch

38

of picturesque romance into the monotonous London streets, where at the turn of the century a foreigner was a foreigner, rarely seen, and always suspect.

[3]

One of the paradoxes of central London, brought to mind by my calling our streets monotonous, is that from Charing Cross one can take a rural walk westwards for some four or five miles almost out to Shepherd's Bush. I know of no other great city, except Paris, that offers this opportunity.

Leaving the railway station, the incredulous countryman is led to The Admiralty Arch that stands back in the southwest corner of Trafalgar Square, and he is thence directed to follow the lengths of the string of parks. For his guidance I wrote, some years ago, a booklet for the Ministry of Works called *The Royal Parks of London*. All the parks leading westward are owned by the Crown and are thus included in that pocket-history.

Admiralty Arch is the butt of The Mall, London's only ceremonial thoroughfare, a level imitation of the Champs-Elysées. On its left lies St James's Park, most Royal of all the open spaces in Town. The eastern end of the Park is railed off from Horse Guards Parade, the back-yard of the Government offices and the picturesque Guard Room and Gateway that face Whitehall. These are our most hackneyed precincts, but no less attractive because of that picture postcard familiarity. The building that surmounts the famous gateway through which Royal processions pass on their route from Buckingham Palace to Westminster Palace and the Abbey is an adaptation of designs by William Kent, who always had a country-house touch in his work. Though dwarfed by our contemporary erections in the neighbourhood, the Horse Guards building is still the centre of that background which, seen from the foot-bridge over the lake halfway along the Park, has a fairytale quality.

The Park was most unfairylike before it came into the possession of the Crown. In the Middle Ages it was the site of a hospital for female lepers, run by the Sisters of St James. King Henry VIII took it in 1532, during the seizure of the monasteries, a governmental procedure similar to that imposed today on the great country estates by Death Duties. It is the oldest of the Royal Parks of London, the others being Primrose Hill, Regents Park, Hyde Park, Kensington Gardens, Green Park, Richmond and Bushey Parks, Hampton Court Palace and Greenwich Park.

The Stuart kings improved St James's; Charles II redesigned it to assuage his nostalgia for Versailles. For this task, he employed the French specialist Le Nôtre, who had artifacted the grounds and waters of Versailles. King Charles laid down a court for the game of *pell-mell* (a sort of free-for-all hockey), and founded an aviary along the

Parliament Square. (Overleaf)

boundary of the Park now marked by Birdcage Walk, which runs from Parliament Square to Buckingham Palace. That privacy of the Palace Garden may now be scrutinized through binoculars from the upper windows and terraces of the several sky-scrapers reared against the royal sanctuary.

St James's Park has a wealthy bird life. It even has a dormitory island (actually an isthmus) at the head of the lake. I once explored it and found it to be thickly lined with droppings. Even the close foliage of the trees and bushes was leprous.

The ducks, the pelican, and the wild birds who are safe there from modern insecticide sprays, offer the illusion of freedom to the Civil Servants who take the air round the lake at lunchtime. W.H.Hudson, who had more love for birds than for human beings, had much to say, through the lucid prose of his *Birds in London*, about their haunts in St James's Park.

The royal vicinity along the northern side of The Mall is rich in palaces. Nash's Carlton House Terrace, on the site of the Prince Regent's extravagant palace, is the southern terminal of what was to have been the boldest, most tasteful adventure in town-planning ever undertaken in London, among people congenitally hostile to such public projects. Nash, with his master's connivance, designed a homogeneous architectural work of art that should begin in the north with the terraces surrounding Regents Park. These were to draw toward Park Crescent, out of which Portland Place marched south to Upper Regent Street, to pass the plan of unity to Regent Street, that swept in an echelon down to Waterloo Place. The original Regent Street built by Nash was a serenely modulated crescent, with an arcade supporting the end building at Piccadilly Circus. The Circus played the articulate part in the junction with Lower Regent Street that a neat elbow plays in a woman's arm.

Most of the dream has gone. At the northern end the terraces round Regents Park have been saved, the war-damaged Park Crescent restored, and parts of Portland Place kept by compromise with modern interruptions, the most aggressive of them being that static ocean liner, Broadcasting House, which towers over All Souls Church, Langham Place, like a hundred thousand ton oil tanker about to ram the *Golden Hind*, Drake's tiny flag-ship, in which he sailed round the world.

Whether we walk along The Mall, or parallel with it through St James's Park, beside the lake, we come to Buckingham Palace. Its bright façade was added early this century, to cover the deep weathering of the original Bath stone. The interior has the character, and quietude, of a great country house, and the general tone is not, as might be expected, of splendour but of modesty, and a habitude of silence. Maybe this is the natural aura of royalty, an office which represents the drawing together of discreet dignity and courtesy, and should therefore be the final signature of a civilized community.

Public life, and what might be called the banners of history, are constantly displayed over these few acres of the royal precincts. I need not repeat what I have already written in the official booklet *The Royal Parks of London* about the riches of this district, and the string of palaces in line with Carlton House Terrace along the right hand side of The Mall as one walks westward.

That walk, which has broken away from my spiral route centred upon Charing Cross, passes in front of Buckingham Palace to the aptly named Green Park, thirty-six acres added by Charles II, to be a 'green thought in a green shade', undulating lawns under trees now heavily matured, with a place for flowers only at bulb-time along the exit into Piccadilly beside the Ritz Hotel.

For the purpose of this experimental country stroll in London, however, I should not take The Queen's Walk (named after Queen Caroline, wife of George II) leading from the Palace to the Ritz. I should follow the footpaths under the trees, to the furthest exit at Hyde Park Corner, cross the end of Piccadilly, and enter Hyde Park. Then, still westward, the walk takes us alongside the Serpentine, or through the southern reach of Rotten Row, to the distant bridge over the lake, and the entrance to Kensington Gardens.

All the way, the character of the parkland is changing. The differences are difficult to place, for in all of them the timber is nobly placed over greensward, and flower beds abound. But the change from Hyde Park to Kensington Gardens is instantly felt, as it were along one's aesthetic nerve. It is like crossing the frontier between two small domains, say from Belgium to Luxembourg. If it is an illusion, I hope the Park Authority will increase it by issuing passports from one to the other, and will demand to see them.

At the further end of Kensington Gardens stands the palace where William of Orange preferred to live, and where Queen Victoria was born in 1819. The sunken garden, with a long ornamental pond surrounded by a covered walk under plashed lime-trees was a haunt of mine when I lived in that neighbourhood for some years between the wars. In those days it was a quiet place, apart from the traffic of the golden carp around the water lilies, and the din of bees in the lime blossom. Sometimes, during high summer, I left home early enough in the morning to be able to sit in that garden for a quarter of an hour, before walking eastward through the parks to my office in Whitehall. Such occasions were a form of Communion, secular maybe, but no less holy than the more orthodox sacrament.

On one of those mornings my solitude was broken by the presence in the garden of an elderly gentleman dressed in an old-fashioned frock-coat and top hat. He raised the top hat as I passed, and I responded accordingly, though with some difficulty because of the flabby condition of my headgear.

Mutually interested in each other's eccentricity in pausing in a garden on a week-day morning, we began to talk, and I discovered that he was a brother of the German painter Max Liebermann. He was one of the many exiled liberal-minded people dispossessed and rejected by the Nazi régime. That fact touched our conversation with melancholy. It was also prolonged, and made me late, so that I had to forgo my walk.

Piccadilly Circus. (Overleaf)

Behind Kensington Palace the semi-private grounds are crossed by a path that leads to Kensington Church Street. A few minutes among houses, across Campden Hill Road, and the pseudo-rural walker turns into Duchess of Bedford's Walk, and the bosky footpath over Campden Hill, to the gate of Holland Park. This is London's latest public park, thrown open since the last war, when Holland House was destroyed; with it the relic of Whig history, and the scene of Lady Caroline Lamb's nympho-maniac adventures.

Before the last war Holland House was still the London home of the old Whig family of Fox-Strangways, Earls of Ilchester. The park sloping away northward ended in dense woodland, railed off at the north-western corner from the crescent called Holland Park, a fine, pompous enclave of large Victorian mansions, each in its own garden. From one year's end to another no human foot trod that woodland, and nothing was done to clear the undergrowth. From my window I could watch the traffic of birds, and squirrels, and listen to the morning chorus and the last flutings of the blackbirds and thrushes through the springtime evenings. A dead, half uprooted pine tree reclined in the branches of neighbouring hornbeams. There it lay, year after year, with an annually new shroud of creepers hanging from its rotting limbs. The scene was one of perpetual solitude, the more melancholy because it was so incongrous with the two main western arteries to south and north of it, Kensington High Street and Holland Park Avenue.

Since Holland House was destroyed, and the park thrown open to the public, a new road, lined with villas, has been cut through the bottom of the woodland, and the neglected corpse of that pine tree has received the last rites.

So too ends the pseudo-country walk which cuts across the spiral pattern originally planned for this book. To return, we can walk over Campden Hill, passing along the top of the Square where the novelists Charles Morgan and Margaret Kennedy lived, near the Reservoir at the top of the hill, the scene of G.K.Chesterton's fantasy, *The Napoleon of Notting Hill*. William Rothenstein, Edmund Dulac, Holman Hunt, and Lord Leighton, four painters no longer fashionable, but famous in their day, lived in this neighbourhood. Indeed, the district comprising Holland Park and Campden Hill has been a cultural colony for over a century, favoured as much as Chelsea by painters, writers and musicians.

[4]

Let us imagine that, in haste to return to our proposed orderly exploration, we have taken a No.9 omnibus back to Charing Cross. That is one of the most delightful rides in London, for it touches the south side of Kensington Gardens and Hyde Park, the north boundary of Green Park, thence through the whole length of Piccadilly to the Circus and down Haymarket to the National Gallery in Trafalgar Square. The trip westward has cut across our plan like the gnomon across the geometry of a sundial. It can also mark a few sunny hours.

Making our way back across Trafalgar Square to the labyrinth of the Adelphi and the little streets that tie the Strand to the Victoria Embankment, we can enjoy the view along the Square to the church of St Martin-in-the-Fields, and across it to Whitehall and the distant prospect of Big Ben, beyond the Cenotaph, both seen through the canyon of Government Buildings, in one of which I spent many purgatorial years, sustained however by congenial colleagues.

Trafalgar Square is comparatively modern. It is another part of the great design of John Nash, to make a more spectacular use of the junction of streets that once stood to the north of the rambling palace of Westminster, of which only Inigo Jones's Banqueting Hall survives, though Westminster Hall, within the Houses of Parliament, may be called a part, indeed the nucleus, of a royal palace whose completion never materialized, owing to the Civil War and subsequent developments of our Constitutional history.

The southern slope of Trafalgar Square, which gives spaciousness to the view down Whitehall, was formerly more marked, but in 1830 Sir Charles Barry terraced the area, to create the level where now the fountains play and minority demonstrations vent the grievances which crop up even in a Welfare State.

On the top terrace stands the National Gallery, designed by Wilkins in the 1830s. It is now too small for its purpose. It has always been severely criticized by architects, who look askance at its dome and its 'pepperpot turrets', but it makes a charming picture when floodlighted at night. I suspect, however, that a couple of juxtaposed dustbins would also become magical under this deceptive treatment.

James Gibbs's design for the church of St Martin-in-the-Fields was so much admired that the plans were used again, to build a church at Mereworth in Kent, though some change was made in the steeple. St Martin's steeple is the symbol of west-central London. It is an aspiration, a signal of the ceaseless Christian activity within the church beneath it. St Martin's has sheltered the destitute in its spacious crypt. It is the seat of memorial services for the famous dead, and marriage ceremonies for the fashionable living. One function after another fill its pews. Its vicars are usually renowned preachers. Dick Sheppard was one of them. His sermons kindled fire, and the recollection of them has kept it alight. In that respect, St Martin's itself is a beacon, drawing everyday life, for a moment, or an hour, out of the surge and uproar of traffic, into a miraculous quiet, which has a traffic of its own, not nostalgic like the interior silence of a country church, but tense and active with a determined purpose, an acceptance of the urban world outside, and a domination over it.

Leaving the church, and standing at the top of the steps under the wide portico, we look along the terrace pavement in front of the National Gallery, toward Pall Mall, to be shocked by the New Zealand building, whose height dwarfs everything in its neighbourhood, and foreshortens Pall Mall. Her Majesty's Theatre beside it on the way

Speakers' Corner, Hyde Park. (Overleaf)

up the Haymarket now looks like a toy palace in a Schwarzwald fairytale, its dome reaching no higher than the fifth storey of the skyscraper. Yet in that dome Beerbohm Tree had his sanctuary, where he entertained proudly, convinced that he was on top of the theatrical world.

The handsome club buildings are also diminished; the United Services opposite, Decimus Burton's Athenæum across Waterloo Place, Barry's Travellers' Club and the Reform (yes, even the majestic Reform). The stately portico of Robert Smirke's Royal College of Physicians (now absorbed by Canada House) has shrunk to the apologetic dimensions of the façade of that little Roman temple to Minerva half sunk into the pavement of the market place at Assisi.

I think of a line from Keats's Ode to the Nightingale: 'No hungry generations tread thee down'. He was referring to the poet's fate, under the hooves of literary fashion. Styles in prose and verse can exist side by side. They do not have to be appreciated simultaneously. But one cannot single out for aesthetic enjoyment the architectural styles of Nash, in his United Services Club, Decimus Burton in The Athenæum, and Barry in the Travellers' and the Reform Clubs, because all are overborne and down-trodden by the characterless bullying of the skyscraper that exalts itself on the site of the vanished Carlton Hotel, the proportionate if undistinguished late Victorian building that harmonized with His Majesty's Theatre next door, and played a modest part in the composition of Pall Mall, at the head of which it stood. Like Romano's restaurant in the Strand, it was a fashionable centre during the Edwardian era, that last decade before the first world war, and the break-up of the worst phase of the Industrial Age, with its ugly economic inequalities, and its garish display of newly acquired wealth against a background, and how vast a background, of squalor.

Further along Pall Mall, on the south side, once stood the Carlton Club, next door to the Reform. Its exterior was Edwardianized belatedly in 1921 by Blomfield, who gave it the character of a period already destroyed by war. Then, in the second bout of war, it got a direct hit from one of a stick of three bombs that also played havoc in Mayfair (King Street and Bond Street). I was 'sleeping' in The Athenæum that night, bedded down in the basement under a billiard table. I remember thinking, amid the inferno of noise, filth and reverberation, 'Ah! This is the end of club life, and all it represents; the cultural enclaves, the professional corporations, the recognizable brotherhoods of merit and achievement, maintained by codes and in circumstances distinctively and uniquely English and Lowland Scottish'. It was a strange thought at that moment amid what seemed to be a tumbling universe. As with most uncontrolled reactions of mind during abnormal physical circumstances, it was probably wrong. Hysteria under fear can take many forms. An exaggerated calmness and detachment is one of them; though that too may be one of Nature's balancing tricks. It may account for many acts of heroism, and self-preservation.

Next morning I picked my way along Pall Mall and saw the shell of the Carlton Club, and exposed behind it the short terrace of Carlton Gardens, where once William Gladstone lived with his parents, at No. 6. The air was still mephitic with brick dust,

Trafalgar Square.

smoke, and the stench of disaster. Pall Mall had become a slum overnight. Again I had a flash of historical consciousness, and saw this picture as a prophecy of things to come after the war, when civilization would be levelled down by equalitarianism, the few numbered with the many, and the many brutalized by the breakdown of all restraints, economic, religious, moral and intellectual. It was a priggish reflection amongst the rubble, the hosepipes and the too abrupt plunge into reality, through the thin veneer which so many of us had thought was a normal way of life.

St Martin-in-the-Fields. (Overleaf)

Further along Pall Mall, beyond the Royal Automobile Club (Edwardian *in excelsis*) still stood the seventeenth-century mansion which was built for one of the members of the Hanoverian Court, named Schomberg. The successful painter Thomas Gainsborough rented it for £300 a year during the height of his fame. Happily it has survived the caprices of commerce; instead of being replaced by a glass-and-concrete block, it has been restored with no external desecration. The caryatids upholding its porch remain, but their invitation is no longer to a social soirée, or to a sitting in the studio. The interior is now a set of neon-lighted offices. No matter, the warm brickwork, the long windows in their William-and-Mary frames, break the increasing monotony of Pall Mall, and offer as it were a grace note to the architectural music of St James's Palace where we enter the precincts of Royalty. The Palace is still the official seat of the Court, and royal proclamations have that address; but it ceased to be the London home of the Sovereign when William IV removed to Buckingham Palace.

Henry VIII built it at about the same period in the sixteenth century as Wolsey built Hampton Court, and the Tudor characteristics of the two palaces are patently to be seen, such as the small Tudor brickwork of the Gateway to St James's. Many alterations and additions have been made by famous architects, Christopher Wren among them. He designed the State Rooms, enclosing them on the south side behind embattled walls. But in general aspect the long, low-storeyed palace remains a Tudor masterpiece, a monument to Renaissance England when she was still an isolated community, startled by her new independence after severing herself from the international hegemony, and the political bonds, of the Roman Church.

Like Buckingham Palace, it holds the interior quietness of a country house. In addition, it has a sense of age, of remoteness both in time and space. It is *petite*, even in the staterooms, and ghosts might comfortably habituate there. So too might a scholar, sufficient within his pedantic enthusiasm, withdraw there into a world of black-letter and vellum, uninterrupted by the twentieth century and the impossible reality of traffic a stone's-throw away, along the Mall and St James's Street.

St James's Street, at right-angles to the end of Pall Mall, and open to the placid scrutiny of the clock-face in the gate-way of the Palace, is a continuation of clubland. It links the clubs in Pall Mall with those along the western half of Piccadilly, facing south over Green Park. Even today St James's Street has an eighteenth-century leisureliness, and motor traffic is an intrusion there.

The oldest of the London clubs survive there, more respectable than when they were founded two hundred years ago as smart coffee houses or raffish gambling dens, where aristocrats were said to dice away their feudal estates overnight. White's, Boodle's, and Brooks's Clubs are the most famous of these, still housed in their eighteenth-century buildings, though that of White's was re-faced in 1852. The house of Brooks's was tidied up after the war, and is a masterpiece of architectural good taste, monument to a period when civilization was an aesthetic rather than a sociological and moral concept.

Other pieces of the period are the two shop fronts at the bottom of the street: Lock

Westminster Hall.

the hatter and Berry the wine-merchant. Their windows, like so many in that fastidious century, have the aptness of design found in that of a violin, or a harp, the very gloves of music.

But my excitement is making me lose sight of my original plan to set out on a systematic walk, spiral-wise from Charing Cross. Again I have broken away, like a child chasing the rainbow. Maybe it is an appropriate and pardonable eccentricity, a sign of filial devotion to the Queen of Cities, as I drag the artist, my willing companion, with me. But at least Charing Cross, by its name, was a good place from which to set out. 'Charing' is said to be a corruption of 'Chère Reine', the name given to the beloved Queen Eleanor, whose funeral cortège was marked by a Cross wherever it rested overnight on its way from the North to London. This charming theory, however, does not explain how the village of Charing in Kent was named.

Byron lived for a while at No. 8 St James's Street, at the time of the publication of the first cantos of *Childe Harold's Pilgrimage* by John Murray of Fleet Street, who was shortly to set up at 50 Albemarle Street in Mayfair, across Piccadilly and only five minutes walk from the rooms where his troublesome but world-famous poet lodged. That story threatens to lead me still further astray across the continent of literary history. I must try to return to my proposed itinerary. I wish I could insinuate the reader

Edwardian Whitehall. (Overleaf)

55

into the upper front room of 50 Albemarle Street, and invite the present John Murray to display the very personal effects of Lord Byron, that onetime darling not only of Mayfair but the whole nation. The original fireplace may be seen, before which the reigning John Murray, a few weeks after Byron's death in Greece in 1824, sat in committee with the poet's executor John Cam Hobhouse and representatives of the family, and solemnly burned the manuscript autobiography which would have revealed the nature of Byron's relationship with his half-sister Augusta Leigh. No doubt it would have had something to say about Shelley's strange friendships, some of them a little less Platonic than his dilated idealism. Had the autobiography been made public, literary gossip-mongers over the past century and a half would have been deprived of much of their speculative estate.

The aroma of that mystery lingers in Albemarle Street today, for people with a sense of history. The street is rich enough in such treasures, for it was here that Michael Faraday, the young genius in physics, developed his work at the Royal Institution, in the heavy-looking pseudo-Corinthian building which sits morosely among the eighteenth-century houses. It consists of three of them thrown into one in 1838, and hidden behind the classical façade by the architect Vulliamy. The interior is gracious, with a noble library and a lecture-theatre so ample and so steeply ranked as an amphitheatre above the lectern and demonstration bench, that the speaker (usually an eminent scientist, but occasionally a man of letters) is liable to a crick in the neck after his discourse of one hour, precisely to the minute.

Further down the Street, on the same side, No. 7 is the headquarters of The National Book League, where bibliographical and other literary exhibitions are staged, and lectures given, above a basement restaurant where a member and guests may eat and drink with fastidious enjoyment after the aesthetic feast in the rooms above, which are intercommunicated by an oval staircase, one of the most handsome in London. In the early nineteenth century the house was a hotel kept by one de Grillon, and it lodged some illustrious refugees from abroad; one of them was Louis Napoleon Bonaparte, later to become the operetta Emperor of France, to the music of Offenbach, and the gate-crashing of Bismarck.

The general architectural mood of Mayfair is eighteenth century, with its squares and elegant residential streets, which I should like to explore in detail, 'had we but world enough, and time'. What little time we have, to wander in this luxurious village, appears to be an indulgent eternity, over-stocked in the shops, arcades, private galleries, clubs and hotels. The invading sky-scrapers, like monstrous Martians, cold and antiseptic, are encroaching there too. The nightingales no longer sing in Berkeley Square, not even in the hearts of septuagenarian passersby on their tottery way to sell an odd volume, long treasured, to Maggs, the dealer in antique books. Even so, the civilized and sophisticated person is drawn toward that concise locality, to the detriment of bank accounts and purses.

58

Waterloo Place, the beginning of Clubland.

CHAPTER THREE

[1]

I have dragged myself back to the centre of my spiral tour, which in theory is to cover the whole of London, gyre upon gyre, as the pigeon plans its flight. Bewildered, after the last outbreak westward, I pause, almost disconsolate, at my failure to go about the task in an orderly disposition of so vast a wealth of material. But I must try again, and resume the exploration where I left it, on the eastern outskirts of the Adelphi, with the intention to move upwards from the River, on the first narrow curve around the Strand and Kingsway, along the beginning of New Oxford Street and the end of High Holborn, then turning down into Covent Garden Market, and St Martin's Lane, back to Trafalgar Square.

The content of that gyre is rich enough, and still richer is the next, wider flight that will include the several Inns of Court, Bloomsbury, Soho, and over the River into Lambeth, Southwark and Bermondsey, on the turn, anti-clockwise, into less publicized and touristicated districts on the widening span, that covers the City, Clerkenwell, Islington, the sinister northern railway terminals with their gloomy Victorian warrens of workers' houses, war-battered and rapidly dissolving into the twentieth-century townscape of international concrete and superficial cleanliness.

Hay Hill, Mayfair. (Overleaf)

All is changing under this latterday metamorphosis, which is sweeping away class distinctions and slums in the one gesture of State benevolence, with an impersonal justice that seems to be having the effect of an anaesthetic on the frustrations and aimlessness of the post-war population.

This wider flight, if not interrupted, should take us westward to Paddington, another neighbourhood painful with railway nerve-ends, to Bayswater, over the Parks which we have already traversed, to Royal Kensington, down to Chelsea, and over the River again to Battersea, Wandsworth, eastering to Brixton and Dulwich.

Within those two further circuits, I should find enough material to fill several volumes, leaving my artist colleague toiling bravely behind.

So let us begin: but first I must try to balance the scheme by moving a little way eastward down-river, after my eccentricities toward the west. Few people can resist the lure of a river, especially when it becomes the purifying lung of a great city, carrying either spring waters from the hills, or from the open saline estuary, accompanying floods of fresh air, and the flotsam remembrances of mother Nature.

Canaletto painted the scene down river in the eighteenth century, from the garden of one of the great houses that stood on the south side of the Strand, with their grounds sloping down to the waterside. He was realist enough to leave a detailed indication of what the great curve round from Charing Cross to Blackfriars looked like two hundred years ago. It seems that the River was much busier as a highway than it is today, though it ran through a city which by contrast with present-day London looks hardly more than an outsize village. Yet a century and a half before Canaletto put this semi-fairyland on record, King James I had spoken with horror of the rapid growth of his new capital.

Now that the tramway has been removed from the Victoria Embankment, the long crescent walk by the riverside from Westminster to Blackfriars may be enjoyed in comparative quiet. The noise made by those trams over the whole of the southern suburbs, and especially during their hiving on the north bank between the bridges, became the characteristic symbol of London during some forty years. Those brown, blunt-ended monsters, their windows olive-green with human breath and tobacco smoke, carried the working-class community to and from its work, by day and by night, with a dour fidelity, for the cost of a few coppers. The fare from Camberwell Green to one of the central bridges was twopence. During the rush hours, morning and evening, the trams were packed with bemused humanity on both decks, the lower deck carrying also the strap-hangers along the central gangway, who swayed like corpses hanging from a gibbet. I recall my own experiences in youth, when I took part in that sardonic ballet every day, clutching the strap with one hand, and holding Whateley's *Logic* or Herbert Spencer's lugubrious *First Principles* in the other, as I tried doggedly to waste no moment of the dolorous journey.

Still in my ears the drum-beat of the syllogism, and the over-positive dogma of Spencer, that stovepipe-hatted philosopher, ring in a dreadful counterpoint to the rhythm of those steel tramwheels over the steel rails, as they screamed and shrieked round the curves, honing the rail edges to razor-sharpness, a menace to all other traffic. The din and clangour ran along the rails and the central channel that carried the electric cable, multiplying the demonstrations of agony until the whole neighbourhood shared the torture. Such was the price London had to pay for this cheap transport in the juggernauts of democracy.

What a grim period that was, during the first four decades of the century, in which the punctuation of two wars was almost a relief from the sordid squalor that accompanied the growth of industry and irresponsible wealth. The sound of those trams, and all that it symbolized in that dreadful period of London's history, its Tumid Age, penetrated into every building, every room, through closed windows and doors; an orchestration direct from Dante's underworld.

After this painful cadenza, played by memory, we can now walk along the Embankment, the River on my right hand, on my left the gardens below the Savoy Hotel and Shell House, then the Temple Gardens, and the private lawns of the lawyers in the Middle and Inner Temple, until I reach the City landing of Blackfriars Bridge.

From that busy junction we move into another London, the City itself, much of it hardly recognizable by people accustomed to it before the depredations of the last war. It was then a medieval city, its caddis-worm structure tied within a network of narrow lanes and alleys, spreading out from the central east-west artery of Cheapside, which carried through eastward to Mile End, and westward to High Holborn and Oxford Street.

The change of scene after passing under the railway bridges at the bottom of Queen Victoria Street and Ludgate Hill is impressive because it affects the mind as well as the eye. The temperature falls, or seems to do so; the rhythm of vehicles and passersby changes, the quality of light and air is different. An element of magic, slightly sinister, carries on back through time to the Victorian age. Yet there is no reason for this. The shops, though fewer, are just as bright and modern as those in the West End. But they are small, of individual enterprise. You will be treated in them as a visitor. So too in the public houses (some of them historical and with literary associations). In spite of the heaviness in the character of the streets and buildings; in spite also of the overcrowding and jostling, the rush and roar of the commercial daytime hours, the visitor begins to realize that he is in a village; he fosters the illusion that the individuals in this ant-heap of clerks, brokers, bankers, solicitors, accountants, Customs and Excisemen, merchants and middlemen, all know each other, habitual in a close relationship that acknowledges itself at intervals in the public houses, the tea- and coffee-shops, for momentary contacts and sometimes over a game of dominoes.

This spirit of intimacy survives, I suspect, along with other anachronisms from the customs, ceremonies, and memorials of the Middle Ages, when the social way of life, based on the mystical dogmas of the Christian Church, assumed that there was a relationship in sin and desperate potentialities among all folk, thus creating a kind of shadow equality and brotherhood, to counter-balance the violent gradings of the feudal system, with all their picturesque differentiations, in housing, attire, food and the rest of material conditions.

In the City of London we find the survivals of the old guilds, structures of ancient crafts and commerce, which combined the functions and responsibilities of our Trades Unions and Employers' Associations, with the emphasis not so much on bargaining over wages, as uniting in maintenance of the quality of work and training of the skilled worker. The various Company Halls such as the Goldsmiths', the Carpenters', the Fishmongers', the Skinners', the Mercers', in all some twenty-two of them, each with its livery, are still to be found within the small area of the City 'square mile'. Some of them, like the Guildhall itself, were damaged or destroyed by enemy action in the 1940s. A few have kept their ancient walls and furniture. The sodality of their members supplies most of the recruits for civic posts, the aldermen and Lord Mayors, whose unique urban parliament, like those of the great free cities within the Holy Roman Empire on the Continent, have maintained the dignity and rights of the City of London since the occasion when the Norman William first tried and failed to subordinate them to the caprice of the Crown.

Much ceremony, or what is called 'custumal', has been evolved to demonstrate the many facets of this freedom. It is still practised today, in the annual programme of the Lord Mayor, during his term at the Mansion House. It is recalled whenever the Sovereign has occasion to enter the City, by the ceremony of the presentation of the sword at Temple Bar, the western point of entrance.

These survivals, though today little more than good-natured and sentimental miming, a kind of fancy-dress ball, maintain the mailed fist in the velvet glove. That glove is liable to be removed hastily should any infringement of the City rights be threatened. Otherwise, the ritual helps to create the atmosphere, that something different, which I have tried and failed to define. It keeps the ghosts walking, and is a perpetual reminder of old challenges, by a small federation of free merchants, to the arrogant claims and conduct of the landed nobles and the almost mystic assumptions to divine right by the Monarchy. The reverberations of those challenges still echo, fainter and fainter, from the vanished walls that once enclosed the precincts of the City.

What is so impressive, in our Age of vast encompassings, too large even to be contained within mother Earth, is the tiny continent of these ancient achievements, and the smallness of their communities. Athens, with its thirty thousand citizens and the dimensions of the Acropolis: medieval England with a total population less than half that of London today, with a wealth of gothic cathedrals, abbeys, country churches, castles and mansions; the proportions put us to shame; our hordes of workers, our slaves the machines. Those ancient craftsmen are anonymous. Are we also different from them as our slave the machine gains ascendancy, forcing us to work under one eponymity, our name Frankenstein, and our future at the mercy of this monster?

Oxford Street, the east-west artery.
East End street cleaners. (Overleaf)

Such wide speculation is so disconcerting that the close confines of the City are comforting. I am eager to lose myself, and the vista of the future, in the narrow streets beyond Printing House Square, whose re-built premises still support the tradition of *The Times*, Anthony Trollope's *Thunderer*, that centre-piece of our British stability.

Opposite, just beyond Ludgate Hill Station, floats the Mermaid Theatre, London's newest. A far-sighted actor named Bernard Miles had a vision of a theatre unburdened by the excessive rentals and overheads that fetter the West End houses. Believing that the changes in contemporary society demanded a new kind of patronage for the arts, he set out to find it. There has to be an aristocracy of some kind for this purpose. Mankind in the mass remains interested only in bread and circuses, or some such primitive equivalent. Bernard Miles turned to the aristocracy of wealth, the City Fathers, and proposed to build a theatre, in the spirit of those Elizabethan houses maintained by Heneage and Alleyn in Clerkenwell and along the south bank in Southwark and Lambeth four hundred years ago, when Shakespear and Marlowe supplied the words, and Burbage spouted them.

Bernard Miles cried 'Unlock your coffers!' Merchants and financiers forsaking the philistine tradition of aldermen, responded generously, in money and kind, such as bricks and timber. And the first play with which this humorous and impassioned actor-manager rewarded them, was the raffish Restoration comedy *Lock up your Daughters*!

The Mermaid has a restaurant at the back, overlooking the River, with its traffic of tugs, barges, coalers, and the little boats of the River Police and Preventive Men. In front, its forecourt is the open junction of Upper Thames Street and Queen Victoria Street. The latter was denuded during the air-raids, but fortunately the College of Arms survived. It is the only historical piece in that otherwise dreary street. It was built in the mid-seventeenth century on the site of an early Tudor mansion, the Town House of the Earls of Derby. It is a charming brick-built Caroline gem, set back on a terrace, with two wings approaching the road.

Upper Thames Street is really the beginning of maritime London and dockland. At once, we come into a world of warehouses, the backs of wharves, hoists hanging from upper floors, begrimed windows, alley-ways down to the River, and cavernous entrances opening upon loading platforms. The litter of packing and unpacking processes blows up and down the low-way, fragrant with pepper, orris, ginger, and waftings from the Orient, so that amid this gloomy scene, through the obstruction of vans and lorries, there percolates an atmosphere of boyish adventure, sailing ships, cutlasses, bandanna headgear and foul-tongued parrots.

It is of course absurd, an olfactory cheat: but it is real enough to anybody making his way along, to reach shortly what once seemed to be an impassible cliff of brickwork. It was the wall of Cannon Street Station, supporting the vast round arch, the biggest in the country. Beneath it, the road, diminished by contrasts, passed into darkness, emerging on the eastern side as Lower Thames Street, to more warehouses and wharves, and widening suddenly, beyond London Bridge, to join Fish Street Hill by the Monument, to become Billingsgate Market.

Here, the romance of the Spice Islands is lost in the sinister stench of fish. At first it is acceptable to the senses, but the saline freshness, as of sea-water, quickly suffers a land-change. It becomes fetid, sickening. Fish porters, in overalls plastered with an oily, semi-phosphorescent accumulation, bustle about, shouting the identity of their burdens, as they seek the lorry or the wholesalers' premises, the load of fish carried on their heads, over a wood-padded helmet, trailing strings of slime whose deposit lies over the pavements, the roadway, the lower courses of the buildings, and even floats, attenuated and horrible, in the air, to the detriment of the clothes and faces of the passerby.

That stench haunts my nostrils still, because half a century ago I had to brave it every morning on my way through the market to the Custom House, the quarter-mile long building that adjoins Billingsgate Market down river.

I frequently cycled there from my rooms on Denmark Hill, braving the junctions at Camberwell Green and The Elephant and Castle, where the interweaving tramlines from east, south and west emerged an inch or two above the worn setts of the roadway, sharp as scimitars, and slippery as eels, waiting to lock the front wheel or rip the tyre off the bicycle. The habitué became skilled in avoiding this danger, and also the relentless indifference of trams grinding along their appointed grooves, unable to concede an inch to the rest of the teeming traffic, whether horsedrawn or mechanical.

The Elephant and Castle junction is the hub of a wheel whose spokes come in from London, Southwark, Blackfriars, Waterloo and Westminster Bridges, to join the roads running south, east and west through the suburbs out to open country. It maintains this function today, as a completely new architectural machine, a most impressive piece of mid-twentieth century town-planning which is likely to alter the social character of the district between the bridges and the southern and south-eastern suburbs.

The bottle-neck was always choked, and the cyclist was rarely able to get through without dismounting and humping his bicycle over the pavements. That may account for my survival, and my reaching the Custom House safely day after day over half a century ago. I stabled my bicycle in a rack, along a dark vault on the ground floor, before climbing the stone stairs to the top of the gloomy Georgian building, where the laboratory occupied the western end, a half dozen rooms, some looking through the top balustrade over the River, others on the northern side giving a view up past the church of St Mary-at-Hill toward Eastcheap.

Every inch of that district, the very core of London City, is a mortuary of historical remains. Turn a stone and you start a Roman ghost. The last such desecration was after the second world war, when the excavations in Walbrook, opposite Cannon Street

The beginning of the Grand Union canal. (Overleaf)

Station, in process of laying the foundations of the present vast office block, revealed the remains of a temple to Mithras. With some reverence, the relic has been re-constituted and made permanently visible within the new building.

The Custom House was damaged during the war, but its famous Long Room, the largest unsupported single span chamber in the country, remains intact. I remember its strange acoustics. Sounds, as well as the tiny human figures scuttling around the floor between the oaken partitioned cubicles and counters, were further diminished beneath the bare walls, that towered up to the curved ceiling, where semi-darkness almost hid the clock and wind-guage. All was smoke-grimed; the smoke of nearly two centuries of commerce, and that invisible miasma rising from bills of lading, manifests, and all the other dusty documents relating to shipping, customs duties and the sinister digestive processes by which a great national State maintains its growth and ensures its survival. Dark and terrifying it was to me, a boy poet, drunk on the illusion of sitting with Theocritus in a remote Sicilian valley, 'piping ditties of no tone' like one of the immortal and immobile figures in Keats's 'Ode on a Grecian Urn'. Never was a squarer peg in a rounder hole. But I have had much to say about that elsewhere, and must pursue my vagary down river.

[2]

Beyond the Custom House, Lower Thames Street leads to Tower Hill, the open mound where City clerks relax at lunchtime, demagogues spout and groups of people with grievances hold meetings. The Tower of London is probably the most visited building in the British Isles, and I need not add to the congestion. The great White Tower which dominates it, has fragments of the Roman wall incorporated in its foundations, laid by William the Conqueror after he came to some agreement with the Saxon citizens of London, on their terms, that he should not interfere with their long-established civic rights, or dilute their freedom with his feudal laws. By building this most powerful fortress of medieval Europe along the line of the Roman Wall, William got as near to the City as he could, without infringement of those rights which he had promised to respect.

For six hundred years the Tower represented the Royal Prerogative over our English way of life, and its threat ended only after the Civil War changed the Monarchy from an absolute to a constitutional authority. The Tower of London is now a wardrobe and a museum, where visitors may see the paraphernalia of the Royal Achievements, used on State occasions such as coronations and the openings of Parliament. Its history as a prison for traitors and persons of high estate who thwarted the caprice of the Crown hangs about it even today, an emanation of the perpetual corruption generated by power.

This association pervades the more decorative and ceremonial aspects of London's oldest monument. The ravens of death, the Traitors' Gate, the Bloody Tower, the execution block, are the symbols that survive in the visitor's memory, poisoning the pleasure to be found in the magnificent romanesque architecture, and all the other accoutrements significant of a millenium of steady growth of national consciousness and civic pride.

The twenty-foot deep moat that once surrounded the Tower was drained in 1843, and it is now a sunken lawn, never, we may hope, to be removed. The action of that formidable hand through the centuries brought mischief and horror into the lives of good and bad people with indiscriminate savagery. Our modern age, with its threat of extinction for the human race either by nuclear bang, or the whimper of starvation as we proliferate like green fly is paradisal by comparison with those times symbolized by the Tower of London.

East of this blood-soaked monument lies dockland. All docks are alike in their happy combination of the picturesque and the squalid, though in London's docks the quality of happiness is hard to find. During the working day there is no opportunity for intro-spection, unless work and its traffic are held up by a strike of dockers. But in the evening the commotion dies down. The narrow streets beyond the Tower, running alongside the river between the cliff-like walls of warehouses, are heavy with an illusory sense of latent melodrama.

But the illusion creates an atmosphere of threat, of something ominous likely to happen as one approaches an alley running down beside a warehouse to the waterside and an abandoned landing-stage. The dilapidated gates loosely padlocked, with gaps where the woodwork has weathered and fallen away under wear and tear; the landing doors above, with the ropes of the hoists tied back to the wall, in the small windows with bleared panes, or stuffed with sacking where the glass has vanished; all indicate rough usage, the jungle of commerce, rougher even than the sea-voyage which begins or ends here. I think of the books of Thomas Burke and H. M. Tomlinson. Burke's *Limehouse Nights* gives a lurid picture of this semi-maritime world; Tomlinson's *Galleon's Reach* is more concerned with the setting than with the human turmoil. I think too of frequent pages in Dickens's novels, portraying the scene further down river, as far east as the confluence of the Thames with the Medway, nowadays a part of the labyrinthine contortions of land and water which carry London's docks down-stream for over twenty miles from Tower Bridge. A useful guide to that labyrinth is a book called *The Widening Thames*, by Robert H. Goodsall, a Kentish architect with a passion for tracing rivers from their springs to their estuaries.

From the top of the Monument in Fish Street Hill, at the head of Billingsgate Market, the view eastward covers London dockland, glimpsed beyond the Tower Bridge, mortised into the Essex and Kentish banks of the Thames, under an elevation of power-cranes and of masts and funnels in ever-changing disposition. It is an awe-inspiring scene, not only in its physical intricacy and verve, but for what it represents:

From High Holborn at night. (Overleaf)

73

the human activity, the vast range and congregation, the wealth and interchange, the endurance over time and circumstance. There it all lies, diminishing into the distance, silent except for the muffled sounds of the work in progress, the rattle of cables, the faint bump of bales or barrels from ship's hold to dockside; and over it all the conglomerate aroma of goods from every part of the world, with tropical spices predominant.

All that, perceived from the Monument, was familiar to me daily long ago when I worked nearby in the attics of the Custom House, where samples of the imports and exports were tested by quantitative chemistry to find their dutiable ingredients. To recall this reminds me also of a poem written many years later, in which I presented that daily habit, and the way a young man's imagination assimilated it. I called it a *passacaglia* because its main rhythm represented the repetitive trudge morning and evening over London Bridge, in the human tide that ebbs and flows every working day. Hay's Wharf, modernised since I first knew it, stands almost opposite the Custom House, on the south bank where Tooley Street comes up to London Bridge approach by Southwark Cathedral.

> Who hasn't heard of London Bridge?
> Who hasn't, at least once in his life,
> Shuffled over London Bridge
> Among commuters by the million;
> Part of that long, black caterpillar
> Nosing northward every morning,
> Slipping southward every night?
>
> There is a myth that bids you wait
> On London Bridge, if you would meet
> With X or Y or the Man in the Moon.
> Sooner or later everyone comes,
> Everyone comes to London Bridge
> And London Bridge hasn't broken down.
>
> But when you are crossing London Bridge
> Southward, homeward, you will see
> Before you on the Bermondsey bank
> A concrete warehouse, square, forbidding,
> With cranes and derricks like antennae
> Hanging over the dark Thames water
> As though some Frankenstein had taught
> His monster to delight in fishing.
> And so he has: the lesson has lasted
> Three hundred years, and the Frankenstein
> Was a Jacobean merchant named Hay.

I've known Hay's Wharf for forty years.
Every sound on a summer's day,
Or under the surly winter dusk,
Comes back to me. And every smell
Rouses a memory of youth,
When coffee berries, orris root,
Nine-and-twenty kinds of tea,
Geranium oil, and oil of pine
Flung their lure across the river
To drug a boy's imagination.

London vanished then, I sailed
Among the Islands of the Blest,
Drifting from East to Western Ind
To land beyond the coral reefs
Where all adventurers have longed
To voyage through the innocent years,
Returning with a cage of birds,
A flaming scarf—a broken heart.

I, and how many argonauts
Cheated by scents from lost Atlantis
Have stumbled home since then, to take
Our places in the shuffling crowd
Morning and evening over the Bridge:
Over the Bridge and past Hay's Wharf,
Past Hay's Wharf with never a glance,
Never a glance and never a thought
Past Hay's Wharf and Over the Bridge,
Over the Bridge and past Hay's Wharf!

The districts that have grown out of dockland have had two features in common, slums and poverty, with which are always associated vice, crime and disease. That association is not the whole story. The inhabitants of dockland took the brunt of the Battle of Britain in 1940 and the dire years that followed. They saw their world, such as it was, brought down in chaos, and they stood up with fortitude and humour, to prove that a breeding-ground so squalid, so degrading, may produce the more

The Guildhall. (Overleaf)

The Barbican, the changing face of the City. (Overleaf)

77

primitive vices, but also the spirit of neighbourliness, and even the more Franciscan virtues, with poverty worn as regalia.

Without the wartime holocaust that destroyed so much of the dockland parishes north and south of the Thames, there would have been no national or municipal authority strong enough to pull down those acres beyond acres of slums, and replace them with homes that are at least sanitary and pride-worthy. The visitor who knew those districts before the last war, and saw the degradation of social habit into which they reduced the inhabitants, recognizes today what miracle the changed environment has worked. Limehouse, Poplar and Bethnal Green north of the River, Bermondsey, Deptford, Greenwich south of it, are parishes that represent this renaissance. Ben Tillett, John Burns, George Lansbury, and other departed spokesmen for these dockland folk, must be reaching down from Elysium to shake hands with Clement Attlee and other social workers whose mission halls and settlements flourished before the wars as the only oases in that social desert. The good work is still needed, but today it is assisted by higher wages and an adequate standard of living. London Bridge has indeed not broken down!

[3]

So much for the view eastward from the Monument. Most visitors on their way to the Tower and to the handsomely restored church of All Hallows, Barking (the Headquarters of Toc H), stop to admire the Monument, which was designed by Christopher Wren and erected some ten years after the Fire of London in 1666. That fire was the most effective sanitary operation ever worked upon a disease-ridden city. But it also destroyed most of medieval London, the wood and plaster buildings, and the noble Gothic cathedral of St Paul's.

Had Christopher Wren been given a free hand over the re-building, as Haussmann was during the Second Empire in Paris, we should have inherited a London of Palladian coherence, crowned by, instead of hiding, the new St Paul's and the host of City churches which demonstrate the genius of Christopher Wren, one of the few people in the post-Classical world who have been able to make all knowledge their province. He stands with Michelangelo, Newton, Leonardo and Goethe. The strange thing is, history decrees that these giants should all be subservient to masters of normal stature, either tyrants, politicians, or committees representing humdrum democracy. So the City of London sprang up after the Great Fire of 1666, as it is re-appearing after the purgation of 1940-45, sporadic, confused, and banal, at the whim of unimaginative individuals, and the intrigue and legalism of financial combines.

The view from the two-hundred-foot column of the Monument looks north-east over Liverpool Street Station, the terminus of the East Anglian railway network. Round about us the rapidly changing aspects of the square mile of the City can be

82

picked out, with the vast area more northward behind St Paul's now filling up with modern office blocks, the semi-skyscrapers whose greater accommodation adds steadily and fatally to the numbers of commuters doomed to the frustration and nerve-strain of daily travel by a traffic-system crowding gradually to a standstill. The great, imaginative reconstruction of the Barbican lies before us, still in progress, though deprived of some of its boldest features.

Turning westward, we see the glory of St Paul's, more fully apparent after the removal of the shroud of soot deposited by three centuries of industrial growth without controlled organization and scientific know-how.

The damage done to the east end of St Paul's during the second world war has been repaired, with a new high altar more in tune with Wren's original design, which was to include a *baldacchino* in the manner of that in St Peter's, Rome. Comparisons between the two cathedrals are inevitable. Both are the prime flower of Renaissance art as applied to the celebration of public life. St Peter's is the larger, but it has a lighter and more lyrical character. St Paul's, though smaller, is more stately, more massive. The structure of the dome, which might be called the *leitmotiv* of London, is a work of mathematical as well as æsthetic genius. I wonder if Wren, while pondering on the problem of stress and strain, sat down to study the construction of the onion, with its layers diminishing toward the core. He decided on three domes, the lowest being seen from the floor inside the building. Through the opening at its top may be seen the middle cone which supports the lantern. The outer dome is laid on a timber frame which rests on the middle cone, under a covering of lead.

Wren gave thirty-six years of his life, amongst other work, to supervision of the building of the Cathedral, from the laying of the foundation stone in 1675, to the completion in 1711. Seven years later he was dismissed from his official post as Surveyor General. Throughout the commission he had been criticized by one body or another, and made to adapt his original plans accordingly. But the Royal Warrant under which he began the work gave him freedom to make such adaptations as he found to be necessary. Political complications always follow such a liberal ukase. The jackals of office were at the master's heels throughout the three decades. He had the character and constitution to survive, however, and he lived to see his cathedral, an oratorio in stone, completed; but not in the open setting which he had planned.

Though today, surrounded by post-war office blocks, St Paul's is once more hemmed in, its grandeur cannot wholly be disguised or rivalled. Distance increases its domination and serenity. Seen from the Monument, or from a train moving between Charing Cross and London Bridge Stations, by day or floodlit by night, it crowns the hill on which it stands, like Authority on its throne. Nor is this power reduced when one looks at the Cathedral set in a panoramic view of central London, seen from Sydenham Hill, or the heights of Highgate and Hampstead. Indeed, its domination grows with distance, and becomes as awe-inspiring as that of St Peter's, seen from the road coming into Rome from Terni, and of that queen of cathedrals, Canterbury, seen from Thannington-Without.

My working day fifty years ago at the Laboratory in the Custom House ended at four o'clock in the afternoon, the hour of Evensong in St Paul's. I used often to hurry at a slow trot that aroused suspicion among the police and passersby, to creep into the cathedral and sit there through the majority of the service. The experience was physical rather than spiritual. Half-drunk upon the self-generated wine of youth, I closed my eyes and had the illusion of leaving the ground, floating echo-borne as the delayed rhythms and cadences of boys' and men's voices flowed over me. My young mind, intimidated by the force and complexity of a world still novel to my inexperience, was restored again and again by this tonic lustration, in a setting so august.

The view westward from the gallery round the base of the dome of St Paul's is open westward down Ludgate Hill and up Fleet Street, broken only by the railway bridge carrying the line from Blackfriars and Ludgate Hill Stations to Holborn Viaduct, the terminus of the old London, Chatham and Dover Railway, a rival in Victorian times of the London and South Eastern Railway whose terminus was Cannon Street. The consequent confusion, obstruction, and wasted valuable building sites still bedevil this region that could be an impressive approach to St Paul's and the heart of the City from the south and west. Holborn Viaduct Station has been given a face-lift after the damage that put it out of commission during the war. Cut into the masonry of its original façade was 'St Petersburg'; an advertising gesture that should be immortalized.

Fleet Street is both a reality and a legend. Its history begins with that of the City, two thousand years ago, as a western outlet, which in the Middle Ages passed through the Temple Gate, beyond the church of St Dunstan-in-the-West. This church today is the symbol of the legendary Fleet Street, the Grub Street of the brotherhood of journalism, an activity which began in the seventeenth century with the gossip writers, such as Thomas Dekker and Nicholas Breton, called 'spies'. They broad-sheeted the news of the day throughout the Town. They were the not wholly reputable voices of Cockaigne, their words hand-set on single sheets, and decorated with crude wood-cuts for initial heading and colophon. Their prose was as clumsy as the type in which it was printed and hawked. But it nourished the widening literacy of laymen, and it quickly improved in range and authority when the first great journalists appeared: Defoe, Addison, Steele, Johnson and Goldsmith. The Fourth Estate was confirmed, and its high-road was Fleet Street.

The man who democratized it, made it nation-wide, world-wide, was Lord Northcliffe, the first Press Baron. He mechanized Grub Street, and converted its hitherto gypsy economics into Big Business. His monument on the wall of St Dunstan-in-the-West marks therefore the historical as well as the geographical end of Grub Street. What replaces it is a highly organized major industry sustained mainly by commercial advertisements, with a few vestigial articulations from the obsolescent world of letters.

Billingsgate Fish Market. (Overleaf)

84

The bust of Northcliffe, in the memorial designed by Lutyens, is a vigorous portrait, by the sculptress Lady Hilton Young, whose first husband was Captain Scott, the heroic explorer of the Antarctic. By him she had a son Peter Scott, naturalist and painter of bird-life. She married later a poet of the first world war, named Hilton Young, who later took to politics, Ministerial office, and the House of Lords.

A *sottoportega* beside St Dunstan's (last survival to remind us that the present church was founded there in the thirteenth century) leads to Clifford's Inn, which with Lincoln's Inn further west, Gray's Inn beyond High Holborn, and Staple Inn at the top of Chancery Lane, stand to the north of Fleet Street, while the Inner and Middle Temples stand slumbering between the top of Fleet Street and the Victoria Embankment, their southern boundary.

These Inns of Court are a medieval establishment, siblings of the universities of Oxford and Cambridge, harbouring post-graduates who have read Law, calling them to the practice of their specialized knowledge, by propounding it in chambers or pleading it in the courts. The profession is as close a corporation as those of the Church or of Medicine. In this country it has a peculiar technical division which tends to be also a social one. On the one side are the barristers, from whom are recruited the members of the Bench; on the other side are the solicitors, who feed the public, either civil or criminal.

This method, in its labyrinthine processes, has worked well over the centuries by keeping the Law aloof in its administration. But for some reason or other, or through some impulse more instinctive than reason, lawyers have always been unpopular and intimidating. During the few riotous outbreaks in English history, some lawyers were lynched. Dickens perpetuated this attitude to the profession in his novel *Bleak House*.

This hostility, so deep-seated in history, and so widely spread in all countries and cultures throughout the world, may be due to the fact that the lawyer is the instrument or mediary by which men and women, under the restraint of civil life, vent their anger, fear, vengeance and hatred, either rightly or wrongly, toward each other. It is a shifting of the sense of guilt on to the shoulders of the person who makes a profit out of our weakness.

Yet the profession has produced, and continues to produce, statesmen, men of scholarship, civil culture in the arts, and especially in that art by which our language is preserved and enlarged. The life work of the late Lord Birkett offers a recent example. For some years in the 1930s I lived in Old Square, Lincoln's Inn; they were halcyon years, because of the courtesy I found there, the congeniality of taste and interests. I recall especially the friendship of one young barrister living in chambers near mine. He is also a painter of impressive ability. His skill as an orator is comparable to that of Norman Birkett, a master of the art. Edward Holroyd Pearce now, as a Judge in the High Court, exercises that skill on the Bench, and in what members of the House of Commons call 'another place'.

Where John Wesley lived in old Barbican. (Overleaf)

Since the Law, as an organism within human society, works largely by resort to precedents, it is bound to be conservative.

This character is reflected in its dwelling places, the Inns of Court. The Temple and Gray's Inns were badly damaged during the second world war, but the restoration, especially that in Gray's Inn, has kept the historical atmosphere. The ghosts of great men have returned, with the exception of that of Charles Lamb, who was born in Crown Office Row in the Inner Temple in 1775. His father, a countryman from Lincolnshire, was servant and clerk to one of the Benchers. Charles spent the first seven years of his life in Crown Office Row, and this early environment moulded a highly sensitive temperament toward a disposition for the archaic, thus creating a balance between formality and an inherited tendency to emotional disturbance. The balance was not wholly maintained, and morbid evidences touch his letters and essays with sinister cross-lights. Many of his letters were written from No. 16 Mitre Court Buildings in the Temple, where he lived during his servitude under the East India Company, a bachelor devoted to the care of his talented but mentally unstable sister Mary, who also occupies a niche in the Pantheon of English Literature.

Crown Office Row was completely destroyed during the war, and the block of chambers replacing it lacks something, that indefinable something, for want of which, I suspect, the spirit of the fastidious Charles Lamb has sighed, turned away, and retreated to Enfield, its last anchorage on Earth: but retreated in vain.

And here am I, still standing by the palisade round the dome of St Paul's, my imagination, like a flight of pigeons, lifting in all directions, to seek familiar footings dear to me. Time as well as space partakes in the panorama. I see other literary figures in the Inns of Court, neighbours, colleagues in the Civil Service as well as in the world of books. Edward Marsh in Raymond Buildings; Harold Nicolson in King's Bench Walk; Frederick Pollock in Old Square, his chambers just below mine, an authority on Spinoza (my guiding star) as well as on international law; Pethick-Lawrence next door to me, that rare bird, a moral and humane politician; Tyrone Guthrie in New Square (the *older* part of Lincoln's Inn!) whose voice is like sword-play, used to magnificent effect in his work as a producer in the theatre. There are other names I want to recall, but I must not count my rosary of private reminiscences from the dome of St Paul's.

[4]

Before coming down to ground level to resume my proposed spiral itinerary, I shall take another look at Fleet Street, rising gradually from the depression of Ludgate Circus. That depression is part of the miniature valley carved by the Fleet River on its way from the source on Hampstead heights, to join the Thames just upstream from Blackfriars Bridge. Unilever House now overspans the spot, where formerly De Kuyper's Hotel stood. The Fleet was once a waterway of importance, when the Thames was London's busiest thoroughfare, but in 1734 it was covered up, and New Bridge Street and Farringdon Row laid along the course, spanned later by a bridge called

Aldgate High Street.

Holborn Viaduct. Further up, the Fleet River remained open until the middle of the nineteenth century, when it still worked a flour mill at Clerkenwell. Michael Harrison deals fully with this story, as with that of the many other Thames tributaries now gone subterranean, in his book *London Beneath the Pavement*, an unique piece of research, as also is *London Growing*, in which he pictures the 'development of a metropolis' from times long pre-Roman to the modern ferro-concrete age.

Panorama from above Billingsgate. (Overleaf)

Fleet Street is romantic only to the outsider, and perhaps to the tyro in journalism thrilled by the novelty of seeing his first reports, reviews or articles in print (even though cut to ribbons). In all its guises, the newspaper world has been swift, ruthless and dangerous.

In the days of its freedom, before Big Business, with the aid of the advertising agencies, took over its finances, it was much more dangerous, as a profession, than it is now. As I hinted above, to be a newspaper man was to be as economically assured as a gypsy, and that meant a life of uncertainty; like that of most poets and novelists, who with the journalist dare to make a living on an acreage of words.

Many provincial newspapers have a London office in Fleet Street, or in one of the lanes and alleys turning off to right or left. These tiny streets, hardly wider than the massive rolls of newsprint constantly being trundled down them from the paper mills in north Kent, have names known throughout the English-speaking world. Who has not heard of Shoe Lane, Bouverie Street, Tudor Street, Bride Lane, Breams Buildings, Bedford Street, Salisbury Square? Maiden Lane, turning out of Bedford Street to run parallel with the top of Fleet Street and ending at Southampton Street by one of the busiest corners of Covent Garden vegetable and fruit market, was the birthplace of J. M. W. Turner, one of the world's greatest painters. His father was a barber in Maiden Lane, near Rules Restaurant where one can still eat English food, as also at the Cheshire Cheese lower down Fleet Street, cooked and served in a way that would be recognized by Dickens, Walter Besant, Edgar Wallace and Philip Gibbs.

When he was a young journalist in Fleet Street, Philip Gibbs wrote a novel called *The Street of Adventure*, about the hazards of life on the Fourth Estate. He dealt further with the ups and downs of a writer's career in a book called *Intellectual Mansions*, his name for a block of flats alongside Battersea Park, fashionable at the beginning of the twentieth century. He lived there, and so did other writers who had to be within hailing distance of Fleet Street and the relentless voices of the editors for whom they slaved. G. K. Chesterton and Adrian Bell, two writers touched by the Divine Fire, also lived there.

Edgar Wallace certainly proved that Fleet Street was the Street of Adventure. He began his career in its gutters, peddling newspapers, the ink on his wares still wet from the presses, his boyish voice half drowned by their roar. He ended up, his name a household word, in debt for over a hundred thousand pounds. A man must have made great wealth to be able to stage such an heroic exit. Courage and lavish generosity are qualities characteristic of the Fleet Street man.

Samuel Johnson, one of the founder fathers of the profession, lived as Boswell describes, 'while the Dictionary was going forward, part of the time in Holborn, part in Gough Square, Fleet Street; and he had an upper room fitted up like a counting-house for the purpose, in which he gave to the copyists their several tasks'. The period

Under the dome of St Paul's.

96

in Holborn was in a house in Staple Inn, behind the Elizabethan façade of shop-fronts in High Holborn looking up Gray's Inn Road.

The house in Gough Square was given to the nation by Lord Rothermere, North-cliffe's brother, who controlled the financial side of the first mammoth newspaper organization in this country, and that 'upper room fitted up like a counting house' may still be visited, and also other rooms where Johnson lived during his penurious years in London, with his elderly wife. She had been a widow, and her sons disap-proved of this second marriage; a frequent reaction of children of a relict. The *European Magazine* for October 1799 records that

'. . . while Dr. and Mrs. Johnson resided in Gough Square, her son, an officer, knocked at the door, and asked the maid if her mistress was at home. She answered, "Yes, Sir, but she is sick in bed". "Oh" says he, "if it's so, tell her that her son Jervis called to know how she did"; and was going away. The maid begged she might run up to tell her mistress, and without attending his answer, left him. Mrs. Johnson, enraptured to hear that her son was below, desired the maid to tell him she longed to embrace him. When the maid descended, the gentleman was gone, and poor Mrs. Johnson was much agitated by the adventure; it was the only time he ever made an effort to see her. Dr. Johnson did all he could to console his wife, but told Mrs. Williams "Her son is uni-formly undutiful; so I conclude, like many other sober men he might once in his life be drunk, and in that fit, nature got the better of his pride".

That picture of filial sentiment gives a human touch to Gough Square, a rather sombre precinct today, hemmed in by later monuments of a now tumid civilization, the equally tumid machinery of its self-expression.

As I make a second effort to turn away from the panorama seen from the dome of St Paul's, I am halted again by the mental and emotional conflict roused in most of us by vast extensions of space or time. These two factors in our lives are like alchemists. They touch ordinary objects with a conjuration of magic. An old newspaper, left perhaps for ten years as lining to a drawer, catches our attention. Its items are no longer daily gossip. They are saturated in nostalgia, and have bloomed with a mildew of music. Space plays the same trick. A person known to us, seen at a distance in open country, is recognized with an overwhelming sense of sadness, of omen. Why is that? Sadness, indeed, seems to be the *Doppelgänger* of extension, both in time and space.

So in looking over London from this height, in the centre of the City, the 'still, sad music of humanity' takes me by the heart. My collaborator in this book must have the same reaction, which I believe to be universal, for so many of his drawings are made from the tops of buildings that offer panoramic scenes. Perhaps we are both trying to escape from the enormity of the scene below; the welter, mile upon mile, year beyond year, out of which it is our task, each artist in his own medium, to induce a pattern representative of the whole.

We escape, like St Simeon on his column eluding the temptations of society, by seeking in these high places for the illusion that we are seeing London, and seeing it whole, reduced to a unit beneath us. It is as well to reproduce some of these drawings from St Paul's, the Monument, from the Hilton Hotel and the new Shell Building on the South Bank. They may excuse our inadequacy.

I have known London since my birth in it more than seventy years ago. Still it is largely unknown to me. Like the fabulous serpent Ouroboros, it is a self-consuming organism, perpetually destroying and renewing its own fabric. The scope of these articulations is too vast for one man's comprehension. He sees changes here and there, in districts and institutions familiar to him, and in moments of enlarged imaginative insight he can appreciate the gradualness of this awe-striking metabolism, the self-maintenance of a great city. Balzac tried to present this dreaded 'wholeness' of Paris; Dickens that of London. Both captured only fragmentary sloughings of this metamorphosis.

What we see from these roof-tops is something that seems unchanging, static. But there comes up from it a deep monotone, like that heard from within a beehive. It more faithfully symbolizes the nature, the entity, of London than does the image lying so passively below.

Dockside scene.

The changes immediately in the neighbourhood of St Paul's are greater than in any part of London, for that area was devastated by the bombing. Various authorities and individual interests are still unable to agree about the re-building, and meanwhile private organizations, few of them concerned with overall æsthetic results, have closed in round the Cathedral, like a degradation of dragons round Andromeda. Perseus is likely to arrive too late.

Paternoster Row was formerly the book-centre of London. It was a typical City lane running alongside St Paul's Churchyard, on the north. In one night of holocaust it was totally destroyed, and with it, the central clearing-house of the British book trade. Many millions of books perished, and few publishers did not feel the loss. This purgation of their lists has never wholly been made good, and where titles have been restored, the choice of reprinting has been dictated by contemporary and fashionable demand. Sir Stanley Unwin, doyen of publishers in Britain during and since the last war, said that 'Trade follows the Book'. More and more today, books follow the trade.

Publishers have deserted the City, with the exception of the great houses of Hodder & Stoughton and Routledge & Kegan Paul, the one in Amen Court, the other in Carter Lane behind Ludgate Hill Station★. The tendency is to shift westward, though Covent Garden and Bloomsbury still harbour many of our leading houses. Since the war some have moved to Mayfair, and as far west as Knightsbridge, which is now London's most fashionable shopping centre for antiques and women's clothes.

The atmosphere of the book trade in Paternoster Row was that of the eighteenth century, when publishing and book-selling was usually a single enterprise, run by an individual on a small scale, exploiting his authors rather as a madame in a bawdy house handled her girls toward the accommodation of her customers. The relationship is different now. Other difficulties and dangers beset the profession of letters, and the publishers who purvey it.

★ Now no longer the case; the Oxford Press moved at the end of 1965.

Westward from the City.

Bow Bells.

CHAPTER FOUR

[1]

The person with a taste for history and the glamour of the past can spend time profitably in the several Inns of Court, whose antique character and customs have survived both bombs and rehabiliation. Temple Church was badly damaged during the war, but the restoration has maintained the original architectural character of the twelfth-century foundation, without repeating the pseudo-Gothic additions made in 1841, exactly a hundred years before the bombing. The circular shape of the church reveals its connections with the Knights Templar, that body of military Christians founded in Burgundy in the twelfth century.

The fact that the Temple in London was contemporary with the founding of the Order is another of the many indications of European unity during the Middle Ages, when the ascendancy of the Catholic Faith (at that time so rightly named) almost succeeded in uniting the sub-continent as a political and religious structure.

Those two elements were incongruous, and the dichotomy was accentuated under the strain caused by the Crusades. 'Politics' seems to be a rogue element, which can never work in harness with other human forces, religion, humanism, aesthetics and technology. It is the member in the committee that conscientiously represents distrust fear, greed and inertia. At the present moment it is rampant, dominating the emergency committee called by mankind to discuss the problems of a world disrupted by the violence of war and the scepticism of contemporary amenities offered by applied science.

Staple Inn.

102

Tucked away outside Temple Church, on a wall enclosing the north side, there used to be a monument to that golden writer Oliver Goldsmith, whose name was apt to his numbers, both in prose and verse. Johnson, who was his good angel, said that he wrote like one. Even the jealous Boswell had to record the following remark by the old curmudgeon, 'Goldsmith, however, was a man, who, whatever he wrote, did it better than any other man could do. He deserved a place in Westminster Abbey, and every year he lived, would have deserved it better'.

Instead, he had a place outside Temple Church, where he was buried on 9 April 1774. It was the nearest burial ground to his chambers in the Temple, where he died, casually attended by his friends. But it is said that 'the staircase at Brick Court was filled, while he lay dying, with the poorest of the city, unhappy ones who have known his kindness'.

Perhaps it was remorse that drove his friends to the promotion of a more conspicuous memorial. Sir Joshua Reynolds selected a site above the door in Poet's Corner in Westminster Abbey, and with the help of the sculptor Nollekens, Reynolds designed the memorial, and Johnson wrote the epitaph in Latin, angrily refusing to desecrate the interior of the Abbey with an inscription in common English.

The new Inner Temple Hall, south of the Church, and the new Master's Lodge east of it, offer recompense for any disappointment one may find in the substitute for Crown Office Row. Repeated visits are necessary, to explore the purlieus of the Temple; the two Halls, the Inner Temple Gateway into the Strand (half-timber work of 1610) through which Shakespear must have passed, for the good reception given to his *Twelfth Night* at its first performance in Middle Temple Hall in 1602 doubtless endeared him to the Benchers.

This Hall is a masterpiece. Fortunately it was not heavily damaged during the war, and the restoration has been discreet. It is a stately example of Tudor architecture (1562–70). The hammerbeam ceiling, and the superb Elizabethan screen, give the Hall a majesty comparable to that of any of the Halls in the colleges of Oxford and Cambridge.

Walking down Middle Temple Lane from the Strand toward the Hall, we pass the entrance to Pump Court on the left. This is a quiet, deeply enclosed court, rather sombre, which leads through to the cloisters and to the Temple Church. These cloisters, which give a monastic environment to Inner Temple Hall and the Church, have one more column since being restored after the war-damage, and now accord with the original plan. They have a pleasing Florentine character.

Fountain Court opens to the right of the lane, and embraces the north wall of Middle Temple Hall, to enhance its beauty. The fountain still plays in the middle of the

Round about St Bride's. (Overleaf)

104

Court, and through its cool veil on a summer lunch hour folk instinctively gather to enjoy the view through to the lower gardens, the Embankment, and the River. Those gardens stretch eastward to the limits of the Inn, and to a gateway into Tudor Street, a sudden transit from the Middle Ages and Dickens land, to the roar of the newspaper world. Tudor Street was once the home of *The Observer, The Referee*, and *The Daily Herald. The Observer* is now housed in the new Times Building in Printing House Square. The other two are dead.

Above this eastern exit runs King's Bench Walk, a noble parade, which has chambered many famous lawyers and judges, and several men of letters. The Inns of Court, however, are now so crowded with barristers that authors have had to be displaced from chambers which they rented 'by grace and favour'. This is another indication of the general contempt shown towards the profession of letters today, perhaps in reaction against the claims made by its critics and advocates in the nineteenth century, when Shelley wrote that 'poets are the unacknowledged legislators of the world'. The unacknowledgement has certainly been perpetuated.

Another gateway to the outer world opens from the western corner of Fountain Court upon an alley in whose angle stands an old public house called The Devereux (the family name of the Elizabethan Earl of Essex whose Town palace stood over this site). Lawyers, authors and journalists have frequented The Devereux for over a century. G. K. Chesterton was an habitué of its grill-room. Though he sometimes celebrated beer in his verse—Fleet Street had a fashion for literary bucolics at the turn of the century, and this included the wayside inn and its honest ale—Chesterton usually drank gin and ginger-ale, perhaps in the vain hope of reducing his Falstaffian figure.

Literary associations may also be found in the nearest of the legal Inns on the north side of the Strand. Clifford's Inn is hidden away behind St Dunstan's Church. The Court was formerly cobbled, and houses stood in a row on the south side, like those on the eastern side in King's Bench Walk. A rather dreary hanger-on of the Victorian literary set, a solicitor named Theodore Watts-Dunton, had his chambers here. He was a vague, unpunctual character, and his office represented his divided interests. Under a quilt of dust, books and documents were accumulated, on the desk, the table, the chairs and the floor. Neither Watts-Dunton nor clients often disturbed this study in still-life. He has won a shadow-immortality by taking charge of the poet Swinburne when that strange, binary genius was about to succumb to his artificially cultivated vices. Watts-Dunton removed him to No. 1, The Pines, on Putney Hill, and nursed him there until he died at a ripe age in 1909, his genius muffled, but his life prolonged.

At No. 13 Clifford's Inn lived Samuel Butler, author of *Erewhon, The Way of all Flesh*, and the *Notebooks*. Bernard Shaw declared that his own prose style, and many of his sociological theories, were modelled on Butler's work and ideas. Both used their literary art to scourge society; and both were careless of the risk that an art loaded with prophetic dynamite is likely to be forgotten after the charge has exploded, and the consequent changes in the structure of society have become familiar.

A publisher in a small way named A. C. Fifield published Butler's work, and later rented the same rooms in 13 Clifford's Inn as an office. He was a gentle idealist, who on principle added to his small list a sociological work by a woman geologist who had specialized in the study of coal, its life-story and its disposition in the bowels of the earth. She was also interested, in an amateur way, in another source of heat, and wrote a treatise on it under the title *Married Love*. It combined sentiment with technical advice upon sexual practice in marriage. Poor Mr Fifield found himself and his author notorious overnight. The book was a best-seller, and Marie Stopes devoted herself for the rest of her life to educating an eager public in the function of sex. She wrote more books and founded a clinic.

The success of *Married Love* appalled Mr Fifield, and he sold the copyright to a more commercially equipped publisher. But the shock had broken him, and he soon left the profession, having sold his imprint to Jonathan Cape. It included the poetry and prose of W. H. Davies, one of the minor immortals.

[2]

Behind Clifford's Inn lies the Record Office, which faces along the lower end of Chancery Lane, and backs on to Fetter Lane. It is one of London's major pseudo-Gothic public buildings, built in the Victorian era, despised by architectural purists, but returning to public favour, because they offer a relief from the stark geometry of the ferro-concrete skyscrapers which now outnumber them.

The Record Office is famous because it houses Magna Carta, the seven-hundred-year-old document which proclaims the sanctity of the individual, and thus legalizes a moral law that Christ first made imperative. The records of the Rolls Court are kept here, as the name of the building implies. Much historical and biographical treasure is hidden in the Rolls, and researchers crawl over them like bees over a bed of prostrate cotoneaster. One such researcher, Professor Leslie Hotson, has been lucky, for while looking for material relevant to some purpose of his own, he has found, by chance, first the documents relating to the murder of Christopher Marlowe, Shakespear's coeval poet; and later, the letters written by the poet Shelley to his first wife Harriet, after their separation.

Almost opposite the Record Office is the dreaded Carey Street, which runs along the north side of the Law Courts, parallel to the Strand, and ends at the Bankruptcy Court. Solace may be found at an ancient public house near a gateway, flanked by period-piece law bookshops, leading into New Square, Lincoln's Inn. One can be well employed in searching for these typical old London pubs, in highways and bye-streets. They are always tiny, squeezed or flattened between or under modern buildings.

Samuel Johnson at St Clement Danes.
At the local. (Overleaf)

110

SAMUEL JOHNSON

We need a guide-book to them, first to help us locate them, in their modesty, and then to point out their idiosyncrasies and outrageous ornamentation. Most of them are rich in Victorian plate-glass mirrors built in to the shelves behind the bar, elaborately scribed in gold-leaf to advertise the wares of brewers and distillers many of whom long ago ceased production. A book called *Guide to London Pubs* by Martin Green and Tony White selects about a hundred of the seven thousand in London and its suburbs.

The social life in these pubs is conservative. The world outside may explode into all kinds of revolutionary experiment, but in the public, private and saloon bars (each a variant of the others) of the London pubs the atmosphere remains unchanged. A kind of subdued benevolence, half-concealing a tolerant discipline, permeates outward from the host, barmen and barmaids. The customers maintain it, with an enlightenment of bush telegraph news that gives the impression of London being, after all, a village where everybody's business is perceived and discreetly discussed, in parenthesis, or by asides, on a vehicle of sub-humour and genial pessimism. A novelist named Patrick Hamilton has captured the mood and the dialogue of this unique world in two books, *Hangover Square*, and *Twenty Thousand Streets under the Sky*. The conversation, desultory and sometimes maudlin, confidential but vague, can be overheard in the wine-dives and the bars secreted throughout the City and the West End, usually in back-streets out of the rush and roar of the traffic, but sometimes in the middle of it, miraculously insulated by the narrowness of the premises where accommodation is but one rank deep, against a bar hung with trophies of the race-course, the music-hall, or some incongruous hobby of the landlord, all displayed overhead against a close background of bottles and cartons, sometimes under a drapery of fairylights.

The serenity, the otherworldliness, as of the psychiatrist's couch, is sometimes broken by a touch of drama. I remember one such occurrence years ago as I was passing the famous pub on an island site, The Elephant and Castle. Suddenly the door of the public bar burst open, and out lumbered a gigantic navvy, more or less in flames of alcohol. Propelling him by prods from the back, was a tiny wizened woman, her hair drawn back and skewered under a man's cap, her apron rolled up around her waist. And with each prod she let out a hopelessly resigned cry of 'Go 'ome, you bleedin' sponge!'

The acceptance of the inevitable implied in this cockney woman's words, with their wry humour, sums up the philosophy of life in the London pub; intermittent, but unchangeable.

I have already referred to the atmosphere within the intimate neighbourhood of Lincoln's Inn; New Square, Old Square and Stone Buildings, set in their two gardens, one in New Square and the other behind Stone Buildings, shut away from Lincoln's Inn Fields by a high brick wall, beyond which is the pavement leading to Great Turnstile and the monstrous uproar of High Holborn, the centre of the main east-west artery through London.

Little bookshops, fast disappearing, are scattered about this neighbourhood between the Strand and Holborn. There used to be one in Great Turnstile just opposite the offices of the *New Statesman*. I once bought there three volumes of the eighteenth-century Hughes's edition of Edmund Spenser's works in six volumes. I paid twopence each for them, out of my weekly wage of fifteen shillings during my first employment as a juvenile in the Land Registry. A year later I picked up two more of the missing volumes at the same price, in Richmond High Street, nine miles away in Surrey. I am still, half a century later, looking for volume six, for this was the edition which Boswell said was praised by Dr Johnson.

Another local find, in the dusty law bookshop under the gateway from Carey Street to New Square, was a first edition of Green's *History of England*. This cost me a shilling, and I paid another shilling to the official bookbinder in the basement of the Land Registry, who rebound my treasure in massive boards with thick, bottle-green leather back and corners, thereby ruining it as a first edition, but preserving it through to my old age, and probably beyond.

Evenings and week-ends in Lincoln's Inn, before the last war, were as quiet as the countryside at that time. Only a faint murmur, hardly more than a vibration, of the consensus of city traffic penetrated to the garden and the chambers. The sluff-sluff of legal foot-leather ceased, and after the gates of the Inn, in Chancery Lane, Lincoln's Inn Fields, and Carey Street were shut at curfew time, nine o'clock at night, no strangers were heard in the precincts. The curfew was rung on a bell given to the Inn by the poet John Donne, a member of the Inn. He brought it back from Cadiz, where he had gone as one of the expedition under the Earl of Essex in 1596.

I could sit in my study, or lie in bed, sunk in divine solitude. Every quarter of an hour, a sprinkling of bell-music flickered over the City, distant, and usually first, from Big Ben, followed by that from the Law Courts near by; then one, two or several in a sweet confusion from numerous churches eastward. And with that interruption of the silence, there rose a flurry of pigeons' wings from the ledges and cornices of the buildings in the Inn, and the branches of the single plane-tree outside my study window.

Often, on a September morning before the inrush of commuters banished the privacy, I went down the eighty-two stone stairs to the garden, where under a certain seat I picked enough mushrooms for breakfast, a pleasant rustic recompense after a night disturbed, perhaps, by the hooting of an owl who lived in one of the enormous plane trees in the Fields outside our garden wall. I record this as another example of the penetration of country things right through the huge urban county, a thirty-mile diameter of bricks and mortar.

Lincoln's Inn Fields is also a quiet retreat, with fine architectural survivals from the eighteenth century on three sides, south, north, and especially west. In one of these period houses the terrifying Mr Tulkinghorn, the solicitor in Dickens's *Bleak House* had his chambers. Dickens knew the district intimately, for he had a short period of

The Law Courts. (Overleaf)

work in New Square. Certain scenes in *Bleak House* present the character of Lincoln's Inn Fields, slightly ominous and intimidating because of the proximity of the Law. Even the charm of the Soane Museum (on the North Side), where once the great architect lived and collected much of the material that now enriches the museum under Sir John Summerson's tasteful care, cannot dispel the sense of restraint that subdues the human element in the Fields. Nor does the presence of the Royal College of Surgeons relieve the tension.

The plane trees in the central garden of the Square are the largest and noblest in London. Their only rivals are those in Berkeley Square further west. London clay, and even London soot, suit the nature of the plane tree, as well as that of the catalpa, and they may be seen, dominant and proud, in our parks and squares.

The first Labour Prime Minister, Ramsay MacDonald, lived in a flat on the north side of Lincoln's Inn Fields, near the Soane Museum. He was then a young married man, his wife Margaret an inspiration not only to him, but to an army of social workers whom she led in the effort to rescue children from the contagion of poverty, during the years before the emergence of the Welfare State. Her selfless character was inherited by her son Malcolm and her daughter Ishbel, both workers for good, behind the scenes.

How bewildering it is, and always has been, to walk from Great Turnstile into High Holborn. Night and day this aorta carries London's traffic-stream, east and west, feeding the lesser arteries with traffic whose daily increase is likely to result in a metropolitan thrombosis. The patient is under treatment on a prescription of one way streets and other forms of control, but a life-saving remedy has not yet been found. The movement of the life-bearing flow grows slower and slower; the poisonous fumes of exhaust gases thicken; the noise of engines creeps up to the limit of endurance. Yet in the midst of this social delirium, a pair of young lovers may be seen, walking along interlocked hip to hip, awe-stricken in the vast solitude of their amour.

Eastward, Holborn takes us back to the City, continuing as Cheapside, which was a Roman road, and then a Saxon road, and so through the centuries as through a fourth dimension, marking this further scale with hoards of antiquarian and archeological treasures whenever the road-surface is disturbed; rings, brooches, ballast, now on display in the British Museum.

Beyond the bridge of Holborn Viaduct over Farringdon Road, and past the Railway Station that still advertises its fellow-terminus, St Petersburg, the highway leads to another great nexus of streets at the Bank of England, having passed the red-ochre Victorian Gothic building by Waterhouse, headquarters of the Prudential Assurance Company, whose agents haunt our doorsteps, and whose capital wealth floods into the furthest veins of London's commerce. A lively contrast is the new building further east, and on the south side, which stretches back along the lane running down to Ludgate Circus. It is an impressive figure of the post-war world, to house the *Daily Mirror* group of newspapers and magazines. This, and other such giant modern structures in the City, inhume many of the old alley-ways and side-streets of medieval London, which by the eve of their destruction during the war had become fetid and nondescript, botched up with characterless, unhealthy office buildings, the out-of-date warrens of a horde of commercial adventurers whose methods were equally out-of-date. Time and the eruptions of history serve London well by this obliteration. But even so, the idiosyncrasy, the architectural caprice that made the character of the City streets so indefinable, are lost in the standardization, inhuman and monotonous, introduced by these vast office blocks.

[3]

Cheapside (where Thomas Hood, the John Betjeman of the nineteenth century, was born in 1799) leads to the heart of the City, the Bank of England. The building was one of John Soane's noblest works, the final signature of the Age of Taste added at the end of the eighteenth century. But the needs of the twentieth century are gargantuan rather than discreet. Our financiers have no column in their ledgers to show the credit of beauty. Soane's Bank building was low on the ground, and what expensive ground! Herbert Baker, an architect of dubious æsthetic sensibility, who had blunted the genius of Lutyens in Delhi, was called in to bludgeon that of Soane in London. He left the outside lower wall of the Bank, gutted the exquisite interior, and piled up a Babylonian erection that already is inadequate from a quantitative point of view. Babylon must haunt the minds of financiers, for the new office block of *The Financial Times*, in Cannon Street, is even more appropriate to the muddy conjunction of the Tigris and Euphrates three thousand years ago, than to the Thameside of our day, where competitive capitalism is in process of being tempered by considerations of public welfare.

From this loud plexus of streets around the Bank, one may turn through the four points of the compass to find famous buildings; the Mansion House, the Royal Exchange, the Guildhall so badly damaged during the war and so handsomely restored since, and the halls of the Livery Companies to which I have already referred. The Guildhall library and picture gallery record the splendour and range of London's history.

Aspiring above these, but dwarfed by the post-war buildings, stand the City churches, most of them designed by Wren to replace the more modest home-chapels maintained by the merchants who, prior to the great Fire of London in 1666, lived 'over the shop', each with his community of family, servants, apprentices and craftsmen.

The Temple Church. (Overleaf)

The towers and spires by Wren which have survived the second holocaust of 1940–1945, are variants of the grace and majesty of his personality, comparable to the music of Handel.

> Towered cities please us then,
> And the busy hum of men,

sang Milton, who was born in Bread Street among those earlier vanished churches. Handel changed Milton's line to 'Populous cities please us then' to fit the measure of his melody. Wren combined the significance of both versions in his restorations, completing a relationship of three masters in three arts, working in affinity of style within the matrix of the Augustan period.

The names of those churches keep their medieval tone. They hang about them like a Crusader's Achievements: St Alban Wood Street; St Andrew Undershaft; St Andrew-by-the-Wardrobe; St Benet Paul's Wharf; St Clement Eastcheap (one of Wren's plainest), St Dunstan-in-the-East; St Edmund the King; St James Garlickhithe; St Magnus the Martyr at the butt and on the level of old London Bridge; St Mary-le-Bow in Cheapside, its bells a true cockney baptism; St Michael Paternoster Royal in College Street where Dick Whittington worshipped and established a college. They can be counted by the score, each with unique features and furniture. Some were wholly destroyed during the last war, but from St Mary-le-Strand in the west, to All Hallows Barking by Tower Hill, these relics of a pious commercial life still punctuate the story of London. Their resident congregations have vanished but on week-days the churches are open to City workers at lunchtime, offering services and sometimes recitals of music.

Monarch of them all is St Bartholomew-the-Great, hidden away by Smithfield Market, and the hospital to which it gave its name. It escaped the Fire of 1666, and the bombs three centuries later, to survive in its Romanesque starkness and austerity as it was built in the twelfth century, when the Augustinian monk named Rahere established a priory and a hospital on the site. The hospital was the first in London, and has maintained its service to the citizens without interruption over eight hundred years. The church is only a fragment of its whole self, for the majority of the nave was pulled down after the Dissolution of the Monasteries, that political and economic process so widely imitated in the twentieth century by Communist and Welfare States hungry for public funds.

The four wholesale food markets in London, Billingsgate for fish, Covent Garden for fruit and vegetables, Leadenhall for game and poultry, and Smithfield for meat, have distinctive characters to differentiate them from each other: but they have one feature in common; it is a gift among their porters for expletive and profane language. But there is no evil intention behind it. Indeed, it is an emanation of good nature and

The New Hall, Lincoln's Inn.

122

All Hallows, Barking, the home of Toc H.

fellowship. A visitor must not be fastidious in contact with it, nor repelled by the equalitarian bonhomie with which he, and even she, is likely to be greeted. I have already described the nauseating stench of Billingsgate Market. Smithfield has its odour also, a fatty, suety reek, with a dubious aftermath as of meat faintly on the turn. Toward the end of the day's work the porters' white overalls have lost their purity. They conjure recollections of the stockyard, or a first-aid station on the battlefield.

All the markets, even the neat demure undercover Leadenhall, finish the day's labour amid a tide of litter. Platoons of scavengers with hose and broom take over, to work amid the sudden silence and desolation.

Billingsgate has the gloomy distinction of the Custom House beside it. Smithfield has a more charming neighbour, the Charterhouse. This began, as its name implies, as a monastery for the Carthusian Order, sited near the medieval City wall. After the Dissolution (our first capital levy) it was put to various public uses. Queen Elizabeth I lived there while her coronation ceremony was being prepared. Early in the seventeenth century it was acquired by a rich merchant named Thomas Sutton, who endowed a hospital, almshouse and school. The school, like the similar foundation in Dulwich, developed into one of our most famous public schools, which remained in the monastic buildings until 1872. The Merchant Taylors' School, hardly less exclusive than Charterhouse, occupied the site until it too was removed into the country. The surviving buildings, round the courtyard garden, have been converted into flats. A resident here, like one in King's Bench Walk in the Temple, can leave his cloistral quietude, and step from the outer gate into pandemonium, the latterday Carthusian into the traffic of Smithfield meat market, the Templar into the roar of the printing presses of Tudor Street.

Living within or near the City offers the comfort of peace at night, as I have shown in describing my own experience. A basis of quietude is surely the only healthy foundation for home life. The late Sir George Sitwell, father of the famous triad of poets, said that every man needed a long picture gallery in his home, where he could combine contemplation with exercise in wet weather. It is a magnificent ideal, increasingly difficult to realize in our small island during democracy's population explosion. Maybe the intrusion of noise, the enemy of philosophic life, is likely to increase until the next outbreak of armageddon, after which the silence will be profound, broken only by the soliloquy of nature, whispering in the ruins.

Meanwhile, individuals who shrink from the increasing momentum of noise, would do well to seek a home in one of these little backwaters in the City, such as the Charterhouse, or the Inns of Court, or on the pent-roof of one of the high modern buildings, twenty storeys or more above the din, St Simeons of the Barbican, or similar elevations.

These musings about a residential return to the precincts of the City are not un-historical, for it is only of late years that this handful of parishes has been reduced to a community of caretakers. Arnold Bennett's novel *Riceyman Steps*, a sombre master-piece in the tone and of the period of the French painter Carrière's portraits, shows the urban equivalent of a village population in the heart of Clerkenwell. Bennett's friend, the novelist Frank Swinnerton, was born there. Mrs Robert Henrey has pictured, in brighter tones, the village life of Shepherd Market, in Mayfair, through several books of her inspired gossip.

The former cheapness of lodgings in the odd corners of the City, in Clerkenwell and Islington, and the nearness of these districts to the British Museum, brought to these obscure hide-outs many people who afterwards have startled the world; I think of the creator of 'Young Italy', the Genoese lawyer Mazzini, who spent his many periods of political exile in London, where he arrived in 1837, the year of the betrayal of the liberal uprising in Europe against the incompetent tyranny of the Habsburg dynasty and the brood of minor monarchies that sheltered under its ineffectual wings. After a third abortive attempt to rouse his countrymen, he came again in 1857 to London, the centre of the British Government whose foreign policy had weighted the balance in favour of the dynasties, rather than of liberalism. After the political skill of Cavour united Italy at last under a comparatively constitutional monarchy, Mazzini continued to use London as a refuge whenever he refused to acquiesce in the compromises by which that monarchy governed the newly formed State.

In his autobiographical writings, Mazzini describes the misery of loneliness during his first exile in London. He had first to learn the language, before he could make a sparse living as a contributor to the *Westminster Review*, the *Monthly Chronicle*, and other liberal magazines. He started a school for Italian children in Clerkenwell. I believe that to this day there is an annual procession in the parish to commemorate the good work done by this great humanitarian during his sojourn there.

These refugees with a social and political grievance during the nineteenth century seem to have chosen the gloomiest quarter of London for their exile. Maybe they feared that the comparative comfort and safety of life in England would ease the chip from their shoulders, and thus relieve them of their zeal for reform and their ardour for revolution. Lenin, Sun Yat-Sen, and Karl Marx lived within moaning distance of Mount Pleasant Post Office, Kings Cross Station, and their secret arsenal, the British Museum Library.

I find Marx the least attractive of these messiahs of materialism. Several times I have visited his grave in Highgate Cemetery, for it is near that which holds my grandparents and my mother. My distant kinswoman, George Eliot, is also buried there.

The Old Bailey.
The Bank of England. (Overleaf)

128

This burial ground is the most picturesque of the many which harbour London's vanished generations. It lies on the southern slope of Highgate Hill below St Michael's Church and the Village. The cemetery is old enough (opened in 1839) to have become draped by time, especially the higher part adjoining the church and the garden of Old Hall. An enclosure of catacombs approached through a pseudo-Egyptian gateway is now overgrown by a luxury of shrubs, grasses and wild flowers. Few, if any, mourners enter, and nothing molests the solitude of this strange retreat, as remote as an Aztec village deserted in the jungle.

Highgate Village is an architect's delight, for South Grove, High Street and Pond Green are rich in seventeenth- and eighteenth-century houses. In one, Arundel House, Francis Bacon died. That house has gone, and on its site stands Old Hall, one of Cromwell's headquarters during the Civil War. Its panelled rooms have sheltered many notable folk since then, among the most recent are the novelist Rumer Godden and the actress Margaret Rutherford, whose work, the one in literature, the other in the theatre, has a quality in common—compassionate humour.

A writer with a sharper bite lived for a while at No.3 The Grove. J.B. Priestley was the second man of letters to inhabit there, for Coleridge preceded him a century earlier, in 1823. He died eleven years later, a hieratic figure whose metaphysical monologues during that last period of his fitful life attracted an audience, many of whose members have also become immortals: Charles and Mary Lamb, C. R. Leslie R.A. (the biographer of John Constable), Hookham Frere, F. W. Maurice and Edward Irving, the last two being divines whose spiritual fire was kindled by sparks from Coleridge's oratory. It was during a walk between Highgate and Hampstead that the elderly Coleridge met and was introduced to the young John Keats. After they had shaken hands and gone their way, Coleridge said to his companion, 'There is death in that hand'. He thus added the gift of prophecy to his other astounding but confused faculties.

The personality of Karl Marx must still be explained, for merely by mentioning him I have been blown off course again. I took this tangent merely to say that the massive stone monument over his grave in Highgate Cemetery is appropriate to the personality it celebrates; heavy, clumsy, obdurate, and wilfully unaware of the minute articulations which make human society so much more subtle, tender and paradoxical than he would permit in his ideal bureaucracy.

Still moving eastward from Holborn and beyond the bounds of the City, we come to the Mile End Road, Limehouse, Bethnal Green, Whitechapel, Stepney and the Sunday market of Petticoat Lane. They are little more than names to a South Londoner, but before the last war these crowded parishes housed a vast mass of the working population, much of it a sweated working population living in slums seemingly irremovable by civic conscience. This dubious part of London, with its companionate parishes in the south-east, took the worst of the assault during the bombing between 1940 and 1944. North of the River, in and beyond dockland, the flat acres were levelled down to worse than their original and natural desolation.

132

Out of the ruins a new urbanity is rising, round the nucleus of the George Lansbury suburb in Poplar. The population is less than half that of the pre-war parishes. Wages and conditions of work have improved, to lift these folk out of a degradation too deep for amateur and religious social missionaries to reach.

Many landmarks, with many endearing intimacies of locality and habit, have vanished in this sudden access of historical change. The silk-weavers of Bethnal Green and Spitalfields, descendants of French Huguenots, have been dispersed. The coster corner-boys of the Mile End Road and its back streets beyond the London Hospital and The People's Palace have given place to a more sinister fraternity of the gutter and the dirt-track. But cockney good-nature, an endemic quality, persists, even under the disguise of long hair, black leather jackets, and the abominable motorbike. Doctors in practice down there can still tell of quiet heroism, of family devotion, of gossips in curlers, rich in the unique cockney humour and powers of endurance, the qualities that emerged during the war and outstayed the bombs designed to destroy them.

[5]

Arnold Bennett and Frank Swinnerton have made a somewhat sinister magic out of the atmosphere of the district between High Holborn and the even more grim environments of what may be called Railway Land; the back streets built in the mid-nineteenth century to house the workers in the marshalling yards and the termini: Kings Cross, Marylebone and St Pancras. No literary skill can lift the gloom from the network of streets entangled round Gray's Inn Road, Clerkenwell Road, Farringdon Street and Rosebery Avenue. Northward to the Angel at Islington the air of depression persists. The poverty may have been diluted since the economic revolution following the last world war, but in general the whole of this quarter of London is a survival of Victorian town growth at its worst. The contagion stretched further, to spread north and west behind the terminal railway stations, round by Euston and out to Paddington, a sad fabric of squalor sinking, decade by decade, into ever more sordid degeneration.

These districts sounded the dominant of depression that became the characteristic and most remembered feature of London during the period between the middle of the nineteenth century and the end of the last war. A few of the more materially and socially fortunate people may have held a concept of London based on Mayfair, St James's and Belgravia. To the majority, London during that period when the Industrial Age was at its ugliest, clumsiest and cruellest, was a metropolis of misery, accurately presented by Bennett's *Riceyman Steps*, the nervously apprehensive novels of Swinnerton and George Gissing, the poem the 'City of Dreadful Night' by the Army schoolmaster James Thomson, and the pictures produced by the Camden School headed by the genius of Walter Sickert.

Mount Pleasant, London's Post Office.

The misery is concise and terrifying, even today, under the mitigation of higher wages and the social responsibilities assumed by the Welfare State. It spread during its virulent period vaguely eastward, poisoning parish after parish, over Walthamstow and Wanstead, almost to the edge of Epping Forest. In a concentrated form it moved northward and then, suddenly, came to an abrupt halt at the bottom of Highgate Hill. Through the railway arch there, the road emerges to Parliament Hill Fields on the left, and the terrace of period houses on the right, the first demonstration of a surviving architectural grace further displayed in Highgate Village where, out of turn, we have already trespassed.

West of Gray's Inn Road, the escape from the acreage of squalor is equally sudden. The walls of the outer buildings of Gray's Inn, though rubbed and greasy along their lowest courses with the contamination, promise style and composure. Inside the enclosure of the Inn, and west of it in Bedford Row and John Street, we are again in the semi-academic world of the lawyers, breathing a simulacrum of the air of the picturesque centuries of the past, whose iniquities and filth we have forgotten.

Gray's Inn suffered heavily from the bombing, most of its central, communal buildings being destroyed. The restoration has been done by a masterly mind, to demonstrate that if the funds are available, our craftsmen in the building trade still have the skill of the medieval guildsmen, and can use it when not frustrated on the one hand by dishonest contractors, and on the other, by the rapacity of the unskilled workers' unions.

Gray's Inn is a legal brotherhood that has existed without interruption for six hundred years. Great men are numbered among its benchers. Thomas Cromwell, who founded our bureaucratic Civil Service, thus filled the gap left when King Henry II failed in the effort owing to the opposition of 'that turbulent priest' Thomas à Becket. An even more persistent Civil Servant, Lord Burghley, was a member of the Inn. Archbishop Laud, Macaulay the historian, and Lord Birkenhead (the F. E. Smith whom Chesterton in a caustic poem invited to 'chuck it, Smith'), are other men of national fame who were trained in Gray's Inn. But the greatest of them all is Francis Bacon, whose system of inductive philosophy dealt a shrewd blow at the Aristotelian doctrines on which the Thomist Catholic Church and the superstitious sciences of the Middle Ages in Europe were built. He gave an intellectual basis to the Reformation, and a *modus operandi* to scientific experiment. We have still to see the final result of this impulse begun by a crafty lawyer who in his lifetime was also Lord Chancellor.

The Hall, which was destroyed during the war, once shared the honours with that of the Middle Temple, in having an association with Shakespear, for in 1594 the first performance of *The Comedy of Errors* took place here.

The last literary and Civil Service connection with the Inn was that of the late Edward Marsh, a great-grandson of the murdered Prime Minister Spencer Perceval.

Petticoat Lane.

Marsh was private secretary to Winston Churchill for some thirty years. He lived in bachelor chambers at 5 Raymond Buildings, in enchanting rooms whose walls, doors and furniture were hidden under water colour paintings by British artists, a speciality in which Marsh was both connoisseur and patron. His room in the Colonial Office in Downing Street was likewise decorated. He was a fastidious littérateur, who edited the several volumes of Georgian poets, his contemporaries; and he translated the Fables of La Fontaine and the poems of Horace with exquisite verbal skill. He was a great dandy, with his monocle, and his epicene voice and manners. He was also a valuable counsellor to any literary aspirant. His judgment operated on a verse, or prose passage, as closely as a surgeon removing an eye cataract, and he did it painlessly.

West of Gray's Inn lies a small neighbourhood of interesting streets, including Bedford Row, an eighteenth-century terrace of houses in use as legal chambers. Every doorway is gracefully decorated with a carved canopy or hood. Further west, and still south of Theobalds road, lies Red Lion Square, where for a while D.G. Rossetti and confederates of the Pre-Raphaelite School, with the poet-novelist George Meredith, lived in a house half-way along the south side.

Bedford Row is continued across Theobalds Road as John Street, another nest of solicitors, and this changes its name to Doughty Street, where Dickens lived at No. 48 at the beginning of his prosperity and his married life. Here he wrote his serial numbers, two novels running simultaneously, while the printers' devils waited in the kitchen for the copy. Biographers have recorded that he got so worked up by this over-exertion of his imagination that sometimes he ran out into the street, weeping and crying aloud, and had to be chased by one or other of the ménage and coaxed home to dinner.

The house is now a Dickens Museum, where sad relics are displayed, as in all such memorial centres; the pens, the spectacles, the snuff boxes, the musical instruments, the cravat and the walking stick, and other husks of glory. I think of Carlyle's house in Cheyne Row, Chelsea, the Keats Museum in Charles Brown's house in Hampstead, the Beethoven House in Bonn. The most poignant touch of all is felt in the handsome apartment where Mozart was born in Salzburg. In a further corner in the middle room is a notice on the wall 'Here stood Mozart's cradle'.

When I saw it I thought of the shepherds who once came to a stable. Of all examples of human genius, that of Mozart stands supreme, in its unaccountable mystery and wholeness. He began as he ended, mature, and went out to the music of his own 'Requiem', perhaps the greatest work of art ever achieved in this world of limited media. And the seedling of it once slept in that cradle. To hoard such relics associated with great men may be pathetic but it is devotional, and helps us to humility and a more sensitive consciousness of immortal values.

Round the corner from Doughty Street is Guilford Street that leads to Coram's Fields, the site of the Foundling Hospital, which was destroyed forty years ago, though the bronze statue of the benevolent Captain Coram survives. This soft-hearted seaman founded the hospital in 1739, to shelter 'deserted infants exposed to the inclemencies of the season'. Hogarth, the artist who so vigorously portrayed human depravity, was an original governor. He persuaded fellow artists to donate pictures for a gallery in the building to attract paying visitors.

Jacob Epstein, the sculptor, once lived in Guilford Street, almost opposite the Foundling Hospital. One could look down from the street into the kitchens of his house, and see the array of copper pans, whose contents contributed so much to sustain the output of that fecund master, whose corpus of work outraged the philistine (who is always with us). In person he was gentle, cordially ugly. I remember encountering him once outside the Home Office, which he had just left in the company of Cunninghame Graham, to whom he introduced me. The contrast between the two men emphasized their singular characteristics: the short, rotund figure of the sculptor, with polished, beaming face, one tooth missing: the long, aloof Scottish laird, gaunt and aquiline. I looked around, expecting to see Rosinante and the donkey tethered to the railings of St James's Park. Epstein's portrait bust of Cunninghame Graham points the Quixotic association.

Costermongers.

Further west, we come to the many survivals of eighteenth-century town-planning. Mecklenburg Square and Brunswick Square flank Coram's Fields to east and west. Thence, we cross Southampton Row into Russell Square, the outpost of Bloomsbury, that continent of the Higher Culture, which flourished at the turn of the century out of the intellectual compost heap of the British Museum. Bloomsbury Square, at the beginning of Great Russell Street, houses the College of Preceptors. Several publishers are officed in Great Russell Street, Bedford Square, and Bloomsbury Street, just as monumental masons are to be found outside the entrance gates of cemeteries. Every trade has its proximities.

The modern central building of London University towers up beyond the British Museum, casting its shadow over Woburn Square and Gordon Square, once the *cor cordium* of the Bloomsbury School of writers and critics. Most members of this group were deep-rooted in the world of scholarship and art. Virginia Woolf and Vanessa Bell were daughters of Leslie Stephen, the Victorian editor of the *Dictionary of National Biography* and of the *Cornhill Magazine*. He too was two generations deep in literary, political and social acquaintance. His first wife was Thackeray's daughter, and his second a Prinsep, widow of Herbert Duckworth. He was also one of the founders of the Alpine Club, and thus helped to establish mountaineering as an associate activity with literary and moral culture.

David Garnett, perhaps the most oddly fecund writer in the group, is the son and grandson of famous men. His mother translated the major Russian novelists of the nineteenth century. His work is strengthened by his scientific knowledge. Geoffrey Keynes, the editor of William Blake's poetry, is also an eminent surgeon. This wide range of intellectual activity is characteristic of the Bloomsbury Group. To converse with E. M. Forster, or Lytton Strachey, was to reach a planet of a different gravitational pull from that of Earth. One returned, perhaps a little disconsolate over one's fallen idols, but purged, purified, and even sterilized.

The influence of the Group may not affect subsequent generations of intellectuals, writers, and painters, but I believe it will tincture our standards of aesthetics permanently, with an astringent flavour that might almost be a preservative.

[6]

Gower Street and Tottenham Court Road, both running parallel north and south between Oxford Street and the Euston Road, seal off Bloomsbury from the western world, though it may be said to colonize in Charlotte Street and Fitzroy Square, where the Higher Intellectual culture is diluted with a somewhat squalid bohemianism, and sullied with miscellaneous wholesale trade depots. But the presence of several first class continental restaurants in Charlotte Street indicates that this quarter is also a colony of Soho, which lies adjacent, south of Oxford Street.

Where Berthold Brecht lived in London.

Soho was the Italian and French quarter of London fifty years ago. Today it is wholly international, with no colour bar. It is compact, within the enclosure of Oxford Street, Regent Street, Shaftsbury Avenue and Charing Cross Road. This is London's Latin Quarter, where crime and occasional outbreaks of violence are engendered in dubious and depressing nightclubs, coffee-bars, and decaying period houses long since lost to respectability. But even in this raffish and often dangerous environment, there are to be found elements of village life, where families flourish through several generations, human flotsam from the pogroms in Russia, Germany, Poland, or political persecution in France, Italy and the Balkans. I remember one such

King's Cross and St Pancras Stations.

One of the hidden pubs.

family from Milan. The parents ran a restaurant called The Commercio in Frith Street, which with Dean Street, Greek Street, Wardour Street and Berwick Street, all running north-south, create the warp to hold the woof of a maze of minor streets threaded across them.

The parents, an elderly couple, were as serious and devout as their daughter, all three members of the Italian church which stands in Soho Square, its chancel butting into the miscellaneous premises of Foyle's Bookshop, claimed to be the biggest bookshop in the world.

The Commercio was not one of the expensive restaurants in Soho. It catered for regular customers, professional people, and the averagely impecunious practitioners of the arts. The daughter, sadly handsome, pensive through heavy-lidded eyes, raven haired and with ivory complexion, was a re-incarnation of Andrea del Sarto's model for his Blessed Virgins. This silent, unassailable beauty must have overheard the conversation of a group of young literary men early in the nineteen-twenties, while they planned, launched and navigated the magazine called *The Criterion*, with T. S. Eliot at the helm.

Soho has been, and is still, a garden for such cultures, which rise unsullied by the vice and degeneracy about which we read in the newspapers, and occasionally get hints of in the street scene. After a fairly close acquaintance with Soho and its gastronomy, over half a century, I have never encountered evil there, or witnessed an act of violence. But I can say the same of my contacts with the dockland of Marseilles, the back streets of Naples, or the slums of Paris. Maybe there is a natural law by which we find what we look for.

The quarter began with the building of Golden Square at the end of the seventeenth century, as part of the westward movement which seems to be characteristic of all urban expansion. Soho Square was laid down at about the same time, on the site of Monmouth House, the home of the unfortunate and illegitimate Prince who so ineffectually headed the West Country revolt against his uncle James II, and the bigotry which proposed to re-establish a Roman Catholic ascendancy in the government of the Realm.

Even in its post-war flower-show transformation, Soho Square has the character of a village green, spread in front of the church, the Italian church built in 1891, on the east side, in Renaissance style, with a campanile. The interior is like that of a myriad churches in Tuscan towns, with its wide apse and its recessed chapels. An Italophil entering it is likely to be overcome with nostalgia as well as devotion.

Soho jazz club.

146

Two small publishing houses used to inhabit the Square, but the one a few doors along from the church disappeared when the eighteenth-century house was replaced by a modern office block. The other lies opposite, across the garden on the west side. Happily this imprint, one of the most discriminating in the profession, still bears this address. Next door, the music publishing department of the Oxford University Press once had its offices, under the direction of a ripe bohemian musicologist named Hubert Foss. Personally controlled publishing houses of this kind, small and idiosyncratic, relics of the early period in the commercial history of the arts, are vanishing. They have always tended to vanish, for their direction has usually been more interested in quality than in profit, like the small West Riding manufacturers in the woollen industry, about whom the novelist Phyllis Bentley writes with intimate knowledge and understanding. Most of the disappearance of these small publishers nowadays is into the maw of big business, to be controlled by statistics and the dictate of the costing-clerk, rather than by enthusiasm and personal aesthetic.

Soho is an appropriate setting for this old-fashioned kind of publisher. It is a centre for small businesses, small shops, small restaurants, each reflecting intimately the character of its owner. The restaurants reflect the nationality of their owners, and thus attract experimental gastronomes, both native and foreign, the English to cultivate a sophisticated palate, the foreigners driven by home-sickness, to seek the familiar French, Italian, Greek, Turkish, Spanish, or Oriental food, as a life-saving alternative to English public catering.

Where Greek Street joins the Square, stands a severely bare eighteenth-century building called The House of St Barnabas. It is bigger than it looks from the outside, for it runs back to a yard and a private chapel added during the neo-Gothic period in the nineteenth century when the house was taken as a hostel for destitute women. It was originally built as the town house of the Beckford family. These were rich traders in the West Indies, whose vast wealth came from many sources, including that of the slave trade. One of the family served as Lord Mayor of London, and he fathered an only son who was brought up in the manner of a royal scion, with private tutors and a corps of personal servants. This pampered offspring grew up to be an eccentric, touched by genius which drove him to grandiose social conduct, such as building gothic castles in Portugal and Wiltshire, where he conducted orgies of pleasure in the tradition of the satanic cults that accompanied the opening phases of the New Romanticism proclaimed by Rousseau.

The young man, whose name was William Beckford, wrote a fantastic tale, in French rather than in his native tongue, called *Vathek, An Arabian Tale*, whose extravagant fancifulness has made it immortal. But it is little more than a belated essay in the Orientalism made fashionable in European literature half a century earlier by Montesquieu, Samuel Johnson, and Oliver Goldsmith.

The fashion followed the wealth that had begun to roll in from the East as the European countries, particularly Britain and France, began to exploit the limitless riches of Asia. Much of the rapid growth of London's commerce and suburbs was fed by this influx. Beckford's originality was illusory. He was only a spokesman of the excessive vulgarity of the new, landless wealth, whose participants produced from time to time these would-be patrons of the arts, and the occasional amateur practitioner such as this self-indulgent verbal fop.

The house where his uncle lived may still be visited. The elaborately plastered ceilings and the fine woodwork have survived the functioning of public Charity.

Greek Street was the scene of a poignant chapter in a work of real genius, as distinct from Beckford's pinchbeck variety. De Quincey, in his book *The Confessions of an English Opium Eater*, told how he was befriended, during starvation days in London, by a young girl whose profession we are allowed to conjecture. During his collapse from hunger she sheltered and nursed him in a room in Greek Street. Then she disappeared, and he never found her again, either to repay her compassion or even to thank her. The remorse gave body to De Quincey's opulent prose, and justified his addiction to long sentences, which he clarified by a masterly use of the colon, one of the most difficult stops to handle with skill.

Opposite The Commercio restaurant (since disappeared) stands a Georgian house where William Hazlitt lived during his latter years; he died there in 1830, his last words

being that he had enjoyed a happy life. This was his puzzling epilogue to a life of cross purposes in art, disaster after disaster in his domestic and amorous affairs, and the burden of a quarrelsome temperament that drove him 'agin the Government' and often out of reach of his friends. He was a good painter, a sane literary critic, and a masterly essayist. In this last he shared a quality with our contemporary J. B. Priestley; the ability to use the essay form without wearing a literary mask. His essays are the voice of a man speaking to men, outside the chamber of the scholar, and away from the editorial desk. It is possible that as time sifts out our human achievements, Priestley will be found to have other affinities with William Hazlitt.

Another painter, of more worldwide fame, lived for a while in Soho, at 41 Beak Street, during 1749–51. He was the Venetian Canaletto, who during that time produced pictures of the Thames on its passage through London. They give the lie to King James I's complaint more than a century earlier, that the use of 'sea-coal' by London's citizens had polluted the air and begrimed the buildings. Perhaps Canaletto chose windy days to work outdoors in the garden below Hungerford Steps, to perpetuate a London riparian scene as enchanting and colourful as that of the Grand Canal in his native Venice.

[7]

Soho encroaches southward across Shaftesbury Avenue and Coventry Street. Restaurants and one-man shops of various idiosyncrasy will be found in the little streets connecting those two high-pressure arteries: De Lisle Street, Rupert Street, Orange Street, Gerrard Street, all lying adjacent to Leicester Square, that centre of the West End which appears to be set solid with strolling humanity for twenty-four hours a day, a tide that welters to and fro between Leicester Square and Piccadilly Circus, unrestrained by the kerbside barriers put up to protect the motor-traffic from the pedestrian.

Gerrard Street, where the poet-journalist John Dryden died in 1700, carries the atmosphere of Soho along to the lower end of the Charing Cross Road, joining it by means of an alley which comes out beside Leicester Square Underground station. Charing Cross Road is the only surviving book-market in London, since the destruction of Paternoster Row in the City. Bargains, and first editions, once upon a time, could be found there in the twopenny boxes outside the shops. That fairytale is over. The whole structure of the book-world is in process of change, both its economy, and the technical methods of printing, binding, and marketing. The book, as an object to be treasured both for its contents and its format, interests only a minority public of collectors, pedants, and rarity-mongers. There are vast new reading publics throughout

On the beat in Soho.

150

the world who know not hard-cover books, and have no place to put them in their living quarters. This is but a facet of the general change in human society, from the static land-bound way of life, to the new nomadic culture, with the vehicle (the car, the aeroplane, the television set, which is a substitute vehicle) more important than the house. Furniture is no longer made to last, to be used in homes, generation after generation. Death duties prevent such endowment, even if it is wanted.

But books can still be found in Charing Cross Road: books old and battered, valuable and worthless, odd volumes and massive uniform editions in calf binding. One shop specializes in the literature of the ballet, one in left-wing propaganda, another in the history and criticism of the fine arts. Every form of bibliophilia may be fed in Charing Cross Road. The student of human nature may also find sustenance there, by watching the people browsing over the book boxes, freely reading at the outdoor shelves, staring misty-eyed at rare editions displayed behind the shop windows. All ages, all nationalities and races, in all conditions of wealth and poverty, jostle together there like winter bees over a honeycomb, unanimous in a lust for print, a passion first fostered by Gutenberg and Caxton some five hundred years ago, and which my old friend Compton Mackenzie believes will be extinguished in another fifty years, when the book will have been superseded by the use of the telephone, the long-playing disc, the radio and the television. Had I not seen the twinkle in his eye as he uttered that prophecy, I should believe that like Othello, 'now my occupation's done', and put down my pen.

I have said nothing about St Anne's, the parish church of Soho, because it has disappeared, except for the tower, which was added to Wren's building at the beginning of the nineteenth century. The tower now dominates a garden which has been made out of the ruins of the body of the church. Before the wars, St Anne's was famous for its organ recitals, and its specialization in the music of J. S. Bach.

Eastward from Soho, beyond Charing Cross Road, the spirit of place changed from Bohemia to Alsatia, for there lay Seven Dials, a nexus of narrow streets converging from Cambridge Circus, Bedford Street, St Martin's Lane, and Long Acre. It had a bad reputation as a cut-throat district, and even after its post-war cleaning up, and the erection of a handsome but sterilizing skyscraper just south of this meeting of seven streets, the junction has a slightly sinister air, as of a backcloth to a Lyceum melodrama.

Here, and nearby round the church of St Giles-in-the-Fields, up to Prince's Circus, the network of back streets, some with blind walls of warehouses serving the overflow from Covent Garden Market, and the printing works of Long Acre, the predominant mood is one of pause, a perpetual lull before a storm that never breaks. People shun these alleys. I remember taking a short cut at lunchtime one day in mid-week, and suddenly finding myself in a pocket of isolation, out of the din and hurly-burly. I turned a corner out of the empty street, and almost bumped into an abandoned hand-

Covent Garden Market.

barrow. Near it stood a fashionably dressed couple, clasped together in a gesture of despair. The young woman was in tears, the man white-faced and agonized. I lowered my head and hurried past, pretending not to see this private drama of two people alone in the whole of the universe.

A few moments later I plunged gratefully into the crowd at Cambridge Circus, the threshold of Theatreland.

Long Acre, which I had left only to meet with this adventure in pathetic mime, borders Covent Garden, one of my most familiar haunts. It contains the stylistic fruit and vegetable market imposed on the square built in 1630 in Italianate piazza form by Inigo Jones, upon the commission of the ground landlord, the Duke of Bedford. The parsimonious Duke also required Inigo Jones to build a church, 'as much like a barn as possible'. The result is the magnificent St Paul's Church, Covent Garden, now the chapel of the theatre world. Its portico, which figures in Bernard Shaw's play *Pygmalion*, is a dignified sham, rather in the manner of a blind window, for it stands at the east end of the church, behind the high altar, and gives no entrance to the church.

The original houses fronting the Square have long since disappeared, and the centre of it has been partially covered in by the iron and glass Market in the style and of the period of the Crystal Palace. Further, the ornate Opera House was built at the north-west corner of the now congested Square. The result is a curious fantasy, something unique in the whole of European urban life. Here is one of the great opera houses of the world circuit, equal to La Scala in Milan, the Fenice in Venice, the Opéra in Paris, the Metropolitan in New York, and the superb State Opera House in Vienna, and the audience has to approach it through a litter of banana skins and cabbage leaves. Almost opposite stands Bow Street Police Station, where drunks and prostitutes are charged, and street revellers bound over. Fruit baskets and barrows are piled high against its walls, and music-lovers hoping for seats in the gallery have to queue down a dreary side street condemned by its situation to perpetual twilight.

But I would not have it otherwise. I prefer it to the grandeur of the setting of the State Opera House in Vienna, the world's proudest palace of Music. I recall the several little 'pull-ups' for vegetable porters, into which the galleryite could hurry for a cup of cocoa or tea served in a thick mug, during the intervals. That dark, cavernous stage door was the entrance to a magic land, where I once saw Melba come out, to be handed into a cab by Martinelli, the debonair tenor to whom, in the anti-climax after that moment, I was introduced by a member of the orchestra, a double-bass player who had been a friend of my childhood years, and who from time to time smuggled me in to rehearsals and contrived to get me complimentary tickets for the first performances in England of *Parsifal* and *Pelléas et Mélisande*, two operas that suffer from lack of dramatic emphasis, not only in their plots, but in their musical structure.

Now, fifty years later, the romantic agonies of Puccini's melodies, and even the more substantial themes of Verdi, are re-awakened in my memory whenever I pass a greengrocer's shop and am greeted by the earthy reek of potatoes, carrots, cabbage,

154

or the Debussy-like whiff of apples. This is only a personal association, but it is worth recording as an aspect of the bizarre geographical setting of Britain's only opera house of international status, still largely run by private enterprise.

[8]

Moving south-west through Covent Garden Market, past a tiny hospital and a cluster of publishers in Henrietta Street and Bedford Street, we leave Garrick Street, with the famous Garrick Club on our right, and return to the Strand and Charing Cross, thus breaking again the expanding spiral of our proposed itinerary. To compensate this centripetal addiction, let us turn back, and walk up Garrick Street, past the palatial home of the Club, whose membership, as its name implies, is composed mainly of men eminent in the world of the theatre. Publishers and writers are also found there, and it is their presence which gives the Garrick Club some affinity with the Savile. Both are situated remotely from the centre of Clubland in Pall Mall, St James's Street and Piccadilly. They also have in common a reputation for cordiality and good food.

Garrick Street, Long Acre, St Martin's Lane, and Monmouth Street join like the spokes of a wheel, confusing to the stranger who may not be aware that Leicester Square, leading through Coventry Street to Piccadilly, lies only a few yards further west.

What more can be said about these two landmarks, publicized in music-hall song, quarrelled over by property developers, the rendezvous of revellers, and recalled through the mists of nostalgia by English folk exiled by circumstance to the outbacks of the world? Even an old heart can glow with simulated warmth at the recollection of plunging into crowd-life there, when to be young was to be intoxicated merely by being alive and noisy.

But what a mediocre setting for the pleasure-haunt of a great city! The significance of Piccadilly Circus in Nash's magnificent town-plan was destroyed early in the twentieth century when his neatly designed Regent Street was pulled down and re-built haphazard in sham Haussmannesque fashion. The Circus is small, enclosed by nondescript buildings plastered with a perpetual display of neon-lit advertisements as indiscriminate as the walls which support them. One island site alongside Shaftesbury Avenue is derelict and covered with hoardings, while Parliament and property-mongers haggle indifferently about the economics of future development.

Meantime, the tide of traffic rises month by month, surging into the ever more in-adequate Circus, with a ferocity only the more concentrated by being channelled through a system of one-way streets. Poor little Eros on his pedestal in the middle of all this din and confusion tries in vain to soar up and out of it. He is the symbol of hope deferred.

Yet one can stand on the circumference of this mælstrom, outside the front door of Swan & Edgar's (the shop at which the immortal Mr Jorrocks proposed 'to get a whole rig-out'), look down the slope of Lower Regent Street, and there, between the handsome buildings of the United Services Club and the Athenæum, beyond the Waterloo Steps and the Duke of York Column, out beyond the Horse Guards Parade and the boundary of St James's Park, see a vista of distances: spires, domes, and roofs, receding into that infinity which takes sudden hold of the human imagination, and wrings it with an anguished longing. A strange experience to encounter, in such an unlikely setting!

But the mind of man is always ready for these adventures in paradox. I remember being one day in the company of an Irish Civil Servant. He was a tall, gaunt and shaggy man, who carried a blackthorn stick as rough-hewn as himself. He was a Greek scholar, and our conversation, or rather his monologue, was about the sequence of plays by Aeschylus, on the misfortunes of the House of Atreus.

We were standing on an island, halfway across the Circus (in the days before traffic lights), hesitant before the next impulse of the tide of 'buses, taxi-cabs, and all the mad miscellany. My companion heeded none of this. He was away on the heights at Mycenae, and the only sound in his ears was that of the sculptured verse of the Greek poet. He peered out of his dim spectacles, and began to chant an antistrophe from one of the choruses in the *Agamemnon*,

> But, oh! when black blood stains the ground,
> And the mortal mortal lies,
> Shall the dead hear when thou chantest?
> To thy charming shall he rise?

This so inflated him that he rose on wings of song, as a means of crossing the second radius of the Circus, to reach the pavement leading to Shaftesbury Avenue, by the little second-hand jeweller's shop. At the same moment the traffic surged forward, snarling like several of the heads of Cerberus, out of Regent Street, Piccadilly, and Lower Regent Street. I seized the Irish classical scholar by his tweed-covered body and hauled him back to the island, and his black-thorn with him. In an instant we were isolated, the tide screaming round us, infuriated by the loss of its prey, like the Furies pursuing Orestes.

My companion looked at me reproachfully, because I had interrupted him, and with added emphasis, by the thumping of his stick on the ground, he repeated the verses, quite unaware how appropriate they were to the present occasion.

So much for the triumph of the human imagination over both space and time, no matter what the circumstances may be during the translation. History, indeed, is largely a record of such occasions.

CHAPTER FIVE

My sense of direction has now become so confused that I begin to despair of keeping to my proposed spiral course. But such a state of mind is inevitable for the wanderer in London. Like the architecture on the back of the caddis-worm, the streets and buildings of London have accreted under the caprice of passing needs and the personalities who have happened to coincide with them. So many of the coagulations of stone, concrete, bricks and mortar have a complexity and confusion outside our human capacity for design. They might have been extruded during some geological upheaval. The collapse into a residuum makes the pattern of London, if it can be called a pattern, that has about it neither rhyme nor reason.

A look at a map of London shows the result of this capricious organic growth. A spider's web, drooping under rough weather, and broken by continuous ingurgitation of victims, is an orderly structure by comparison with London's mesh of streets. It is impossible, therefore, to be consistently methodical when exploring them. The effort would distort distances and imperil significances. I intend to turn south from Piccadilly Circus, following the dream conjured by that view from Swan & Edgar's front door, and to let my subconscious attraction carry me where it will. Let us see what comes of it.

There is not much to be said for Lower Regent Street, except that being a slope, it offers the prospect which has beguiled me. I submit, and make my way down to the eastern end of Pall Mall, and turn westward along it, into the clubland of St James's and ultimately to the urban village of Mayfair.

No sooner have I taken this direction than I realize that I am re-treading a side-issue already taken in this now bewildering itinerary. So I dodge round by Marlborough House at the end of Pall Mall, and pass Inigo Jones's Queen's Chapel, whose stark wall abrupt on the pavement hides a richly ornate interior.

Entering The Mall I walk along to Buckingham Palace, leave the land of ceremonial by the archway into the road named after the Palace, and pass the Royal Stables and picture gallery. The neighbourhood of Victoria Station and coach terminus is interesting only as a means of getting away from London, and is therefore outside our present purpose, though a walk should be taken for a few hundred yards up Victoria Street (formerly the most depressing street in central London, but now being enlightened with modern office blocks at the top end, near the precincts of Westminster Abbey). The purpose is to visit the only major Byzantine building in London, the Roman Catholic Cathedral, built early in the present century by the architect John Bentley. The interior is still in process of being clad in marble, with decorative detail gradually piling up. When the cathedral was first put into commission, the interior was bare brick, and the effect of this was a magnificent austerity, more evocative of Divine Authority and the Noumenal Creator, than is the bric-à-brac which screens the more conventional congregation from so formidable a Presence. But all this is a matter of personal taste; one person's mode of worship is another person's blasphemy. From an aesthetic point of view, the bare skeleton of Bentley's brickwork made the interior of the Cathedral an architectural masterpiece.

The most impressive of the embellishments are the Stations of the Cross by Eric Gill, the sculptor and typographer whose art has tended to purify and stylize the fine arts in Britain during the short period between the abominable Edwardian *art nouveau* and the latterday dominance of the constructional engineer, even in the art of sculpture. Gill was a convert to Roman Catholicism, and became a tertiary of the Dominican Order. He was certainly a great teacher, as well as practising artist. But his principles were acquired in boyhood, spent in Chichester, where his father was a verger in the Cathedral. In Chichester Cathedral there are some Saxon monumental tablets whose likeness to Gill's work is startling: it might be called the art of pure line, an engraver's inspiration. Some good examples of it may be seen on the decorations scratched on the stone of the pulpit in the re-built *Dom* in Munich.

Unfortunately, Westminster Cathedral is hemmed in behind the Army & Navy Stores, off Victoria Street, and long ranges of expensive flats, called Ashley Gardens, built in that *art nouveau* style which I have deplored above.

Out in Victoria Street, a tablet will be seen on the wall of an equally depressing block of flats opposite the world-famous Stores. It commemorates the versatile com-

Westminster Cathedral.

poser Arthur Sullivan, who produced not only *Iolanthe*, but also the hymn 'Onward Christian Soldiers'; not only the incisive comic opera *Patience*, but also the lush ballad 'The Lost Chord'.

The district covered by Victoria Street between Westminster Abbey and Victoria Station was formerly a slum area. I cannot understand why slums are usually found nestling round great religious buildings. It may be that in the Middle Ages, when the Church offered comfort in a world of hideous mischance and cruelty, and physical sanctuary in its precincts to the unfortunate and criminal, these social misfits and their descendants gravitated there.

Such areas were lively enough, and the cheap market in Stratton Ground which turns off Victoria Street, is the western boundary of the cluster of streets below Horse-ferry Road that contained this rough-house district. It is all gone now, and the new Westminster Hospital occupies much of the area, a more spacious one than its former site on the approach to Parliament Square.

Stratton Ground leads to the Grey Coat School for girls, established in the eighteenth century, in the building destroyed by bombs during the war but gracefully restored to its petite beauty. Beyond this charming relief from surroundings of depressing squalor, we encounter another oasis, Vincent Square, now the playing fields of Westminster School, and the home of the Royal Horticultural Society, where garden lovers attend the seasonal shows, much to their discomposure over their own efforts at home.

Moving towards the Abbey precincts from Vincent Square, we find Westminster School, partly housed in some of the residential buildings of the Abbey, along one side of Dean's Yard. Here one is in the midst of archeological relics and the ecclesiastical and scholastic world. The atmosphere is one of grammar and black-letter, but the visitor must beware of tripping over a pair of football boots.

The only other redeeming feature of Victoria Street is that it leads, through Broadway past Caxton Hall and the Headquarter Building of London Transport standing over St James's Park Underground Station, to Queen Anne's Gate and Petty France, a continuation of Tothill Street under the clifflike shadow of the first of London's blocks of flats, Queen Anne's Mansions. Queen Victoria protested, as at an act of *lèse-majesté*, when she saw this primitive sky-scraper looming over St James's Park. She feared for the privacy of her palace garden. What would she say today, now that several erections, so much higher and so much nearer, have finally destroyed the mystique of royalty, to make the monarch almost as approachable as an American president?

Petty France, once a quiet backwater with an antique furniture shop, now holds the Passport Office, and is thus incorporated in the colourless corridors of bureaucracy.

Queen Anne's Gate is the final attraction that has induced me to walk up Victoria Street. There is not much of it, and its houses are mostly occupied as the offices of consulting engineers. But the row of houses, on both sides of the little close, is a perfect example of eighteenth-century domestic architecture, even more stylistic than those

160

in Bedford Row. Those on the northern side back, with small gardens, onto Birdcage Walk, with access to it, and to St James's Park, down the curved alleyway of Cockpit Steps, a name which tells the history of this approach to one of the vanished sports once enjoyed there.

[2]

Victoria Station sprawls like a flung shawl over the approach to another seamy district, Pimlico, to its right-hand, and to the stately suburb of Belgravia, on its left-hand. Pimlico was not originally so subfusc as it is today. Its terraces of large town-houses once sheltered Victorian middle-class families, with servants in basement and attic. Pillared porticos, symbols of commercial affluence, survive today, but now they disguise the sub-let rooms within; the 'bed-sit', the gas-ring, the shared water closet and the common bathroom; these, and other properties of the anonymous man, and woman, rubbing along as best they can, inadequate and ignored, in our acquisitive society, the small trash in the moraine ground out by the pressure of that glacier.

But like the slum areas of the East End, Pimlico is gradually awakening to a new respectability, especially in the area contiguous to the River, alongside and behind Grosvenor Road, which is an upriver continuation of the Victoria Embankment, broken only by the placing of the Houses of Parliament. The great tower of the Vickers building marks the change. It stands on a site that formerly held a row of large villas, in one of which lived Beatrice and Sidney Webb, who loomed over the socialist Fabian Society like Scylla and Charybdis, threatening all comers with their fanged statistics.

Until this cleaning-up began, that bank of the river between Lambeth and Vauxhall Bridges kept some small survivals of the old riparian picturesque landing stages and moorings which can still be seen in Canaletto's London paintings. Great settlements of modern flats, the first of them being Dolphin Square, the largest in Britain, and possibly in the world, now lie alongside the River as far as Vauxhall Bridge Road. Here may be found the twentieth-century way of life, largely indifferent to a background of privacy and solitude. The balcony is part of the living quarters, and the car waits below, to carry the tenants at week-ends to the caravan site or the country cottage by the sea or in the shires, from which solitude has also been banished by the road house and other demonstrations of the Affluent Society, which floats like a bubble yet to be pricked.

More directly behind Victoria Station, Buckingham Palace Road, containing the huge motor-coach station, and the terminal of the B.O.A.C. (a more contemporary

The seat of the Government. (Overleaf)

The crypt, St Stephen's (Overleaf)

House of Commons, West façade. (Overleaf)

gateway out of Britain), skirts the northern side of Pimlico, whose boundary here is the railway line. A short way along the road, a turning to the left bridges the line and cuts through the centre of Pimlico, emerging at the foot of Vauxhall Bridge, to join the A20 route, which runs straight to Folkestone and Dover via Maidstone, the capital town of Kent.

Thus Pimlico is sealed off, but it is becoming increasingly popular among higher Civil Servants and Members of Parliament, because of its proximity to Whitehall and the House. The tinkle of the Division Bell can almost be heard along Grosvenor Road and in Eccleston and Warwick Squares.

On the other side of Buckingham Palace Road, behind Grosvenor Gardens which lead along the wall of the grounds of the Royal Palace to Hyde Park Corner and St George's Hospital, Belgravia spreads in grandeur and comparative quietude. Belgrave Square lies behind the hospital, and beyond it, Lowndes Square. These, with Eaton Square, provide flats in Town for the aristocracy and landed gentry who formerly maintained houses in Mayfair. Belgravia is august and expensive. It is also rather dull. But the skilful conversion of the huge houses in Eaton Square by coupling two, with a horizontal break through, is much to be commended. The only drawback is the noise of traffic along the centre of the Square, which is a main artery out to the south-west, via Sloane Square and the King's Road, Chelsea.

A more intimate part of Belgravia lies behind Belgrave Square, whose mansions are mostly occupied by organizations and embassies, though Lord Howard de Walden, that last aristocratic patron of the Arts, maintained a Town house here until 'all but he had fled'. The voluntary body that runs hospital libraries throughout the country has its headquarters, and re-binding work rooms, in one of the mansions. Tattered paperbacks are re-conditioned there, to emerge between hard-board covers looking like medieval missals or breviaries, to be loaned around the wards. A hospital visitor might be deceived into the belief that the patients have become devout as a consequence of their suffering, though they may be reading one of the sadistic fantasies of the late Ian Fleming.

Buckingham Palace Road ends just beyond the B.O.A.C. building, at a fork composed of Pimlico Road and Ebury Bridge Road. Nearby is Ebury Street, immortalized by three artists who have lived there, George Moore, Edith Evans and Noël Coward. George Moore knew the other two as infants there, and was the first to recognize their talent, and to encourage it. In his old age, Moore was visited in his house in Ebury Street by a devoted younger generation of writers, some of them perhaps hoping to be given the secret of his second period prose style, in which he developed a kind of

Westminster Abbey, a forest of Stone.
Westminster Abbey from the Victoria Tower. (Overleaf)

168

smooth-running verbal counterpoint devoid of paragraphic structure. In his earlier books, such as the two impressive novels, *A Mummer's Wife* and *Esther Waters*, he wrote under the influence of Huysmans and Zola, and even in his later preference for literary musing and the re-telling of tales from Irish mythology, the realism learned from these French masters occasionally peeps out with a malicious glance. There he sat, until his death in 1933, a slippered and unbuttoned oracle, composing his *Conversations in Ebury Street*, and thereby adding another thoroughfare to the fabulous but indestructible City of Letters.

Winding through a maze of streets we reach Sloane Square from the south, instead of more directly from the east through Eaton Square. North of it lies the rest of Belgravia, which merges into the Knightsbridge area, of expensive residential streets and squares, massive and Victorian, mostly built by Cubitt, who believed in solidity rather than in grace. The majority of the houses are converted into flats, and so are the groom's quarters in the mews behind each street. The earl's daughter now lives over the Bentley.

West and south of Sloane Square the village of Chelsea still remains intact. For a period between the wars its fame as the artists' quarter of London faded, before the greater incandescence of Holland Park and Campden Hill. In this it was like Montmartre which suffered an eclipse by Montparnasse in Paris. But the root of Chelsea's fame was too deep to be destroyed. The plant was set in the sixteenth century, when Thomas More lived there, a monarch of the mind and the spirit of Man, surrounded by his family, and visited by scholars from all the universities of Europe. Erasmus was the greatest of them. These two humanists stood out amongst the noblest figures in the pageant of Renaissance Europe, when a weary and time-soiled polity and religious system began to be put to the test of a new kind of enquiry, as a purgation. Much of it was conducted in the family circle, in Thomas More's house and garden in Chelsea. In 1527 Holbein made a drawing of this family group, which may be seen in the gallery in Basle.

Thomas More possessed that quality of spiritual genius which combines an unshakeable faith with a powerful, relentless sceptical intellectual probing. All books speculating about the future are based on his book *Utopia*. Religion as we see it reforming itself today, in an environment of scientific analysis, must in its new acceptances work towards a definition of truth very much in the way that More made his synthesis, of an orthodoxy relieved of the burdens of politics and superstition.

Sir Thomas More's home, a country house in large grounds, covered the land around the approach to Battersea Bridge. It is now crossed by Beaufort Street, which takes its name from the palace built on the same site by a Duke of Beaufort. The artists' quarter of Chelsea lies between Beaufort Street and Flood Street. It is dominated by the old parish church, a Gothic building destroyed by enemy action in the last war, but now rebuilt, to incorporate the fragments that lay about for some years under a shroud of willow-herb, old man's beard, and other memorial vegetation brought by the wind, the birds, and other spirits of compassion, to assuage 'man's inhumanity to man'.

172

Newton's tomb in Westminster Abbey.

The tiny village community of narrow streets in this area runs up from the River to King's Road, the continuation of that great artery which carries the traffic south-westward right out of London. My father as an infant came with his mother from the countryside at Woburn, to live first in Markham Square, then in Danvers Street within a few yards of the parish church, just around the time of the building of the Embankment in 1874. He had a famous neighbour in Cheyne Row, who had been settled there in childless domesticity with his wife Jane for fifty years. I have elsewhere described the encounter of Thomas Carlyle with the small boy who had been sent by his mother with a basin to buy a few ounces of pickled onions. He spied the figure in the wide hat, long Scottish coat, and serviceable stick, who shuffled along, muttering to himself. The temptation was too great. A pickled onion took flight, and found its mark. She-bears were called down by the old prophet, to punish such irreverence, but my father was more fortunate than the children who mocked at Elisha, for the stick was shaken at him in vain and no she-bears devoured him. He escaped untouched from his first, and last, contact with the world of letters.

The holocaust spared Sir Thomas More's chapel in the old Church (All Saints), and this may still be seen, with many other monuments rescued from the ruins and replaced. They include tablets to Henry James the novelist, and William de Morgan, the associate of the pre-Raphaelite group, who specialized in designing and manufacturing tiles in his workshop in Chelsea, and at the age of sixty began to write the novels which made him widely known. The churchyard was sentimentally picturesque, with its urns, tombs and gravestones moss-clad by time and weather, and draped by ivy and creepers. Since the re-building, the graveyard is more cared for, and has a municipal rather than elegiac air. But the monument to Sir Hans Sloane, a great character in Chelsea during the eighteenth century, can still be seen. Sloane, a pioneer in medicine and the study of natural history, was a member of the Royal Society, and its Secretary. Later, he succeeded Newton as its President, and was the first doctor to be given a baronetcy. He bought the manor of Chelsea to house his vast collection of books, manuscripts and bric-à-brac, the material which he left to the nation as the foundation of the British Museum. Part of his Chelsea garden was bequeathed to the Apothecaries' Company, and is still known as the Botanical Garden, where the annual Flower Show is held.

Chelsea developed rapidly during the nineteenth century, and a second parish church, dedicated to St Luke in deference to the memory of Dr Sloane, was built in Sidney Street in 1824, in the manner of the Perpendicular period of Gothic architecture, which may have begun to show some self-consciousness, but nevertheless carried with it an exultation. This is demonstrated in the lofty St Luke's Church in Sidney Street. In the mid-century its vicar was a man named Gerald Blunt, a cousin of

Middlesex Guild Hall.
Victoria Station. (Overleaf)

174

hofbauer

the minor poet Wilfrid Scawen Blunt, who was made an honorary sheikh by the Arabs, and bred Arab horses on his family estate near Horsham in Sussex. The Blunts, a large family, have since been closely attached to Chelsea, and Reginald Blunt is its most readable historian.

That history is much associated with the arts, especially during and since the nineteenth century. The connection began in the days after the Restoration, when Charles II's Nell Gwyn housed herself comfortably in the smaller village of Fulham. That accounts for the name of the King's Road, which is really Chelsea High Street. It is now one of the most traffic-bedevilled roads in London, maddening to both motorist and pedestrian, though it keeps its bohemian and sophisticated character. It has a music-hall; a Town Hall frequently used for exhibitions of paintings; coffee bars and restaurants; several delightful residential squares such as Royal Avenue, and Markham, Wellington and Paulton's Squares. Shops displaying period furniture and antiques abound, but bargains are not likely to be found until the seeker approaches the shabby quarter known as the World's End, a cluster of semi-slums round Lott's Road Power Station, which looms gloomily like a gigantic fourlegged stool, to signpost the boundary between Chelsea and the now featureless suburb, Fulham. At the turn of the century, however, Fulham also housed a number of artists, mainly around Parson's Green, halfway between Lott's Road and Putney Bridge, at the foot of which is a small riverside park and Fulham Palace, the official home of the Bishop of London.

The little streets running down to the Embankment from the King's Road, are the most authentic artists' quarter of London: Flood Street, Manor Street, Old Church Street, Danvers Street, Tite Street, and the alleys connecting them. They lie west of the Botanical Gardens, Ranelagh Gardens (once a famous playground that rivalled Vauxhall Gardens) and the Royal Hospital which still has its Army Pensioners in their uniform of the Wellington period.

The catalogue of famous parishioners is a long one. Thomas Carlyle spent most of his cantankered married life in No. 24 Cheyne Row, a small street connecting the riverside Cheyne Walk with Upper Cheyne Row and on to King's Road. William de Morgan made his pre-Raphaelite pottery and tiles at No. 34. Leigh Hunt, an older contemporary of Carlyle, lived for seven of his restless years round the corner in Upper Cheyne Row. He wrote his immortal lyric about Mrs Carlyle during this neighbourly period.

> Jenny kissed me when we met,
> Jumping from the chair she sat in;
> Time, you thief, who love to get
> Sweets into your list, put that in!
> Say I'm weary, say I'm sad,
> Say that health and wealth have miss'd me,
> Say I'm growing old, but add,
> Jenny kissed me.

178

The floating population of Chelsea Reach.

He was indeed old, and no longer the vigorous Radical editor, friend of Keats, Shelley and Byron. A later generation of literary giants saw him only as a loquacious old sponger; but there was still a light in his eye, and that disinterestedness which so often makes spongers irresistible.

Cheyne Walk became the centre of the pre-Raphaelite Brotherhood, when its most dominant member Dante Gabriel Rossetti settled in No. 16 in 1862, and filled his garden with exotic animals, and his house with friends, George Meredith and Swinburne among them. George Eliot lived in the Walk during the short term of her legally married life to a young man named Cross. Maclise the painter and friend of Dickens lived there. So did that genius, one of the greatest of European artists, J. M. W. Turner. But he was a miserly man, grubby in person and matter-of-fact in his sexual life, combining it with the services of his charwoman, who cleaned his studio at the further end of Cheyne Walk, a site however where he could see to advantage the symphonies of sunrise and sunset along the gamut of the River-waters.

179

The Thames takes a curve here, round Chelsea Reach, thus creating an isthmus on the other, southern bank. It is called Battersea, and is to me unreal, a fantasy, because it was my birthplace. This must be the reason, or un-reason, why I am again lured away from my spiral course. There are certain mysterious elements in our blood which emerge actively from time to time, like hurricanes out of the Sargasso Sea, to batter and flood the buildings and furniture of our conscious minds. We erect safety barriers of will-power, of logic, and throw out bastions of duty, prudence, and a sense of social justice. Suddenly the whirlwind comes. We call it instinct, if it is evil; intuition, if it is benevolent. For these visitations are not always destructive. Here is one such that does no mischief; the lure of a birthplace.

The Battersea into which I was born in the 1890s was not an earthly paradise. It was built on marshy ground, within the curve of the River, to house humble folk; working class and lower-middle class, many of them immigrants from the impoverished countryside, or but one generation away from such migration. There was no Welfare State. The trade unions were still sullenly battering at the gates of oppression. Society was a free-for-all. Many of its failures and victims lived in Battersea, nursing their rejection and hoping in vain for better times.

Revivalist religions provided a medicine. Chapels abounded in those back streets, which surrounded the tiny riverside village at the crown of the isthmus. The little parish church of St Mary in that cul-de-sac of maritime character, was built in the eighteenth century on a religious foundation eight hundred years older. This parish, with the manor house which survives today, had been the seat of political Henry St John, Lord Bolinbroke, who had an association with the French Court of Louis XIV, through marriage with a niece of Madame de Maintenon, the King's morganatic wife, who was famed for her piety and moderating influence on that wanton and extravagant environment.

[3]

We lived in a little house almost under the shadow of the spire of a Roman Catholic church, the centre of a seminary and school. My parents, who fluctuated between Church of England and Congregational, with short excursions into Primitive Atheism, were consistent in warning us of the dangers lurking in that Roman enclosure. I avoided it on my way to and from school, and read threats into the duet of the two bells that rang from that spire at unaccountable intervals every day of the week. I looked for signs of depravity among the children who attended that Catholic school. How sad it is to recall those scenes, the grim Victorian age of superstitions, prejudiced insularity, the filth of the industrial age powered by coal and steam, the low wages still based on the concept of feudal servitude.

Chelsea Embankment.

Yet amid all this, one child at least lived in a state of ecstatic fervour comparable to that which animated the poet and engraver William Blake, who had lived in the same parish nearly a century earlier, evolving his fantastic private mythology, based on a naïve interpretation of the teachings of Swedenborg, and illustrated by pseudo-classical drawings and paintings imitative of the more sophisticated craftsmanship of Flaxman.

The Battersea that I knew, insular and costive with near-poverty, pervaded by the rancid odour from Price's Candle Factory, still maintained a character faintly reminiscent of a seaside fishing village; something saline, bleached, as of old ropes, hawsers, scrubbed woodwork. Women holystoned their doorsteps. Husbands put up masts in their back-yards, perhaps to guide the homing flight of their pigeons. Heavy fogs cut us off from the rest of the world in winter; and in summer gigantic sunflowers a foot in diameter nodded at neighbours over the fences that marked the bounds of our Englishman's castles.

All is changed there now. Everything is freer, cleaner, more dynamic and communal. But gone with the jealous privacy of the family circle is the pride of possession that maintained those Victorian homes, with every stick of furniture sacred, under the last vestiges of a mystique surviving from a Puritan England, out of which, as by paradox, latterday democracy has sprung, aggressive and irresistible.

Battersea Park, a municipal and not a royal enclosure, has kept the lush quality of the riverside meadows from which it was made in the 1850s. It has noble elm trees, a boating lake, a soft-surface ride for equestrians, and a delightful riverside walk. When I was a child, at the period when the bicycle was a novelty, High Society from over the River used the circular road in Battersea Park as a track. Grooms wheeled the bicycles to the Park, to await the arrival of the ladies and gentlemen in their carriages. The bicycles were mounted, with the aid of the grooms, and for an hour or more the toffs (as the aristocracy was called in those days) pedalled round and round the Park, enraptured by this new form of constitutional exercise. Then, after the cyclists dismounted, the carriages reappeared, the nobility drove away, and the grooms wheeled the bicycles out of the Park.

This was a short-lived comedy on a stage that had formerly offered more serious drama, such as the duel fought between the Duke of Wellington and the Marquis of Winchelsea in 1829. It is said that both Julius Caesar and the Emperor Claudius forced their way across the Thames at this point during their campaigns to subjugate the native Britons.

Battersea Park is celebrated for its festivals. For many years its annual chrysanthemum show drew enthusiasts from all over the country. I remember, as a child, staring face to face at great blooms as big as my own head, marvelling at the symmetry of those cultivated petals, reared under the rules of some floral geometry beyond my puerile comprehension.

Since the Festival of Britain in 1951, part of Battersea Park has been cordoned off as a Fair Ground, with appropriate noises and crowds. The more peaceful amenities of the Park, such as the opportunity for a 'green thought in a green shade', have been banished, and the tenants in the Prince of Wales Mansions (the scene of Philip Gibbs's novel *Intellectual Mansions*) have protested in vain against a development so characteristic of a community ever increasing in numbers, affluence and leisure.

I remember the Park as it lay nearly seventy years ago, quiet in the summer sunlight, the giant elm trees slumbering in their own shadow, a few boys playing cricket across the open ground, their cries far away, accentuating the silence, the murmur of the air in the foliage, the whisper of the water lapping over the mud below the river wall after the passing of a tug-boat with barges. I spent eternities on that promenade, busy in my miniature universe, while my mother sat, her face shaded by a straw hat called a 'boater', clicking the moments away with her crochet needle, her wrists making little jerky spasms that worked upon my infant imagination like endearments, and made her all the more adorable.

South-east from Battersea, to Clapham, and south-west to Wandsworth, the flat ex-marshland rises to the higher ground which is the rim of the saucer containing London. To the north stand the heights of Hampstead and Highgate, which look

Battersea. (Overleaf).

south, across the flat panorama of the vast city, to those of Clapham, Wandsworth, Denmark Hill and Sydenham. Hidden between the two last lies the tiny paradise of Dulwich.

But before I leave Battersea, I must recall the glory of the three bridges that approach it. Chelsea Bridge, which replaced a predecessor in 1934, offers in its unadornment an amusing contrast to its upstream neighbour Albert Bridge, a cat's-cradle suspended over the river so delicately that it trembles under the stamp of a horse's hoof or the throb of a diesel engine. Its balustrades are cut by small openwork portholes, through which a child can peer at the water below.

From here, and also from the more solid Battersea Bridge further up-river, may be seen winter, early springtime and late autumn sunsets reflected in the stream. The spectacle has attracted artists as a candle-flame attracts moths, usually with as disastrous results. But a few masters have captured the magic; Turner, Peter de Wint, the American Whistler. On the first day of the twentieth century, my brother and I walked over Battersea Bridge, intent on an important juvenile mission, and as we hurried furtively from the Chelsea foot of the bridge (such being the nature of our adventure) the four o'clock drama of the sinking sun confronted us. We saw him go down in a panoply of flaming mist. The river caught fire. The stone of the bridge turned rose-red. I saw my brother's lurid hands and face and the crimson in the whites of his eyes. The normally grey building of Mayhew's Flour Mill flushed like living flesh. Those few minutes during which we crossed the bridge were fused into permanence, to stay with me for the rest of my life. They have given me an understanding of the genius of place, and an alertness to recognize it wherever it may be demonstrated; and that is everywhere. In Shakespear's historical play, Henry IV Part 2, Falstaff advances to the footlights, holds up a flask of canary sack, and cries that it is 'an inflammation'. So was that one sunset which flared through my infant mind and made it incandescent, with a light which still serves me.

[4]

Crossing Battersea via a road junction called The Latchmere, we climb out of this hollow by a street called Pig Hill, to the genteel parish of Clapham, now a villa-clad district round a little common consisting of few acres of grass. Edward Thomas, the literary journalist killed in Flanders during the last phase of the 1914-18 war, was posthumously discovered to be a poet whose verse had an elusive beauty comparable to the music of Scriabin, carrying a wayward melancholy combined with a close attention to nature, the moods of the English countryside, and the delights of solitude. I was amused to read, in a biography of Thomas written by an American, that the poet and his future wife enjoyed the transports of love, far from contact with humanity, among the wild groves of gorse on Clapham Common!

If it were possible in so confined an open space, such conduct would have shocked

186

the ghosts of certain earlier inhabitants who had lived in the stately villas along the North Side of the Common. Even that of Samuel Pepys would have looked askance, for he came to live there late in life, long after the confidential indiscretions recorded in his *Diary*. He died there in 1703. The august period, however, matured a century later, when North Side housed the Clapham Sect, a group of rich Evangelical moralists (they were too stiff-necked to be called Christian) led by William Wilberforce, who combined piety with politics, fought for the abolition of slavery, and carried their bill through Parliament in 1807. Two members of the group, Zacchary Macaulay and James Stephen, in addition to their own contribution to our English regal assurance of the freedom of the individual, enriched a later generation with descendants of even greater achievement, Thomas Babington Macaulay as an historian, Virginia Woolf as a novelist, Vanessa Bell, her sister, as a painter.

Clapham Junction Station is a huge, windy railway complex, where the trains coming in from south-west England are channelled through Vauxhall into Waterloo, the terminus. Somewhere in his self-pitiful and over-scented writing, Oscar Wilde describes his misery while he waited on Clapham Junction Station, in the company of warders, on his way to prison.

From Clapham we can drive cross-suburb eastward to Brixton, at right angles to the main roads coming in like spokes of a wheel to the hub, from the Home Counties. There is not much to be said for this cluster of inner suburbs round the conjunction of the large boroughs of Wandsworth and Lambeth. Brixton Hill, Herne Hill, Camberwell Grove, suggest by their names a certain variety of scene, and relief from the flatness of the greater part of these boroughs in their approach to London and the Thames. Kennington, in Lambeth, is famous for the Oval Cricket Ground. Joseph Chamberlain once lived in Camberwell Grove.

Brixton is a dormitory headquarters for professionals of the theatre and music-hall. If one has to think of Brixton, Stockwell, Wandsworth, one thinks simultaneously of 'lodgings', the respectable landlady, the aspidistra, the 'off-licence', the racing news and *The Era*, now defunct, but for many years the journal of the profession. Changes in economic life are sweeping away much of that picturesque raffishness, along with the costers and pigeon fanciers of Battersea, but these elements of our urban society have not entirely disappeared. The folk portrayed by George Belcher, Pett Ridge, Neill Lyons, and by Somerset Maugham in his first book *Liza of Lambeth*, are still to be found amongst the older inhabitants of these southern parishes, fending off the indignities of circumstance with a querulous humour and a pride that during the Battle of of Britain when London burned, was not to be distinguished from heroism.

Still wandering away southward through those inner suburbs that used to be so dreary; mazes of monotonous streets of Victorian villas, seedy from age and the near-poverty of the average folk inhabiting them, we see how post-war alterations in our social and economic structure are reflected in the changes that have brightened up these districts, especially round the road junctions that punctuate absorbed village centres, and over the rebuilt areas devastated during the war. Tall blocks of flats signify a different way of life from that of two generations past in the terraces of dwellings, some semi-detached, all with a yard at the back, fenced-in to ensure a pretence of privacy. The modern villas are frequently set in planned groups, an architectural syncopation pleasing to eye and mind: indoors, no back kitchen with its cast-iron range, and a lean-to scullery beyond, where the cold tap drips into a slate or earthenware sink. Labour-saving, generously served with windows, power-points and automatic heating, these latterday suburban homes may be infamously expensive, flimsily built, and much too few, but for the housewives and husbands able to secure them, they bring a degree of aeration into everyday life such as their grandparents had to seek with more deliberation and effort of will, in religious faith and mansions of the mind.

The parishes beyond Clapham, over Wandsworth Common, are Balham, Tooting and Streatham, hardly distinguishable from each other. Tooting Bec has another small common, where pet dogs and babies may be exercised by bored elders. Streatham, however, has the distinction of a charming little park on a hillside looking south toward the open Surrey country. It is a sort of Boboli Gardens, with that character common to all such terraced retreats. It is good to recall, also, that two hundred years ago Samuel Johnson probably stumbled around those acres, when he was the frequent guest of Mr and Mrs Thrale, who had their country villa nearby, in a delightful rural setting, a complete contrast to their London home by the Southwark brewery, which made and maintained the family fortunes. It is still there, and can be seen beside the railway line between Waterloo and London Bridge stations. I wonder if Messrs Barclay and Perkins have, in the brewery office, any relics of Dr Johnson's respect for the generous and scholarly Mr Thrale, who used to sit there?

Wandsworth includes all these parishes, for its was the largest borough in London before the reorganization of the county government in 1964, when the familiar initials L.C.C. were expunged from our everyday life, just as our concept of the Trinity would be were Britain subjected to an atheist régime. Putney and Roehampton are also part of Wandsworth, but by the time we have reached those outlying suburbs, maybe on our way to the Wimbledon tennis courts, the influence of London has thinned out, and we might be in any provincial subtopia. Putney Bridge, however, has character with Fulham parish church and the Bishop's Palace and riverside garden at the north approach, and Putney Parish church at the south. The road over the bridge continues up Putney High Street, crosses the Richmond Road, and rises up Putney Hill to the beginning of Wimbledon Common. At the foot of the hill, on the left-hand side, is a row of Victorian villas. At No. 1, The Pines, lived Theodore Watts-Dunton as self-appointed guardian of the middle-aged to elderly poet Swinburne, who submitted with surprising docility.

The wing-clipped genius, however, took a daily walk up the hill to the little public-house (still in commission) at the top, on the edge of the Common, drank a tankard of beer, and walked down to The Pines to resume his book-worm activities, and an occasional outburst of verse-making, usually in dramatic form, and a hollow echo of the sonorous music which had made him a major poet in spite of, rather than because of, its content. It is said that during these daily constitutionals, Swinburne had a habit of peering into babies' prams, eager to enquire of the new arrivals as to their journey to earth, and whence they had come. But there is a similar legend about Shelley committing the same imbecility while walking over Magdalen Bridge, Oxford. We may suspect it as a generalization, by a philistine world, to illustrate the supposed eccentricity of poets.

Wimbledon Common, beginning as an upland open space, dropping south to Richmond and the Surrey countryside (now sadly suburbanized but still graceful with its downs and sandy, birch-clad commons) carries us outside the boundary of London. But Richmond Park, Bushey Park and Hampton Court Palace are easily within the scope of the London explorer, and information about them may be found in the booklet *The Royal Parks of London* published by H.M. Stationery Office.

Nearer Town, Kew Gardens lies beside the Thames, on the Surrey side, and it has a magic beyond compare. Even its imitation Chinese pagoda can be accepted as part of the paradox of this fairyland set down amid prosaic suburbs, with an untidy stretch of riverside industrial mess opposite along the north bank of the River. The groves, the individual trees and bushes, the flower beds, and the wonders of tropical vegetation in the glass-houses, the botanical museum, and finally the courtesy and helpfulness of the learned staff, make Kew Gardens a paradise for a day—and many another day of perpetual surprises throughout the year. A pair of lovers keeping a tryst there will be tempted to forget each other for a while, and they will succumb to this healthy diversion of their raptures.

Kew Green, outside the gates of this earthly paradise, is a survival of a typical English village green, with period houses still in private habitation on the further side. Those backing onto the River are mainly occupied by caterers providing teas for visitors to Kew Gardens.

Chiswick Mall, and Hammersmith Mall further down river on the north bank, are two oases in the desert. The new overhead motorway leading to London Airport and the West Country has sliced open those flat western suburbs and robbed them of geographical identity. The traveller leaving London for the West will recognize the museum land of Kensington while driving along Cromwell Road. After that, he rises on a ramp into futurity, a world of concrete and roof-tops, segments of villadom and greenery. He might be leaving any megatropolis in the New World, if the ferocity of the motorcade allows him to let imagination wander for half a second.

Several of the handsome old houses along Chiswick Mall have had their gardens narrowly shaved by the new fly-over, but the character of these few hundred yards of Thameside is still unspoiled. The tide ebbs and flows round the tiny islet of grass and

Street Market. (Overleaf)

willows lying off-shore. Sometimes a spring tide overflows the roadway along the esplanade, and fills the basement floors of the houses, although some have permanent barricades of concrete in lieu of railings along the pavement.

The Mall, with the parish church at its west end, has many biographical associations. Walpole House is particularly rich. Barbara Villiers, Duchess of Cleveland, one of the more predatory of Charles II's mistresses, spent her last years in this house, and was buried in the churchyard near by. Horace Walpole lived there before settling in Twickenham. The house was once a preparatory school and Thackeray went there from his home in India. I wonder what tortures he suffered: were they as unendurable as those which Dickens said he experienced as a child, when he worked in the blacking factory by Hungerford Stairs? Actors, authors, artists of distinction live in other period houses along Chiswick Mall, and most of them give an annual houseparty in spring on Boat Race Day, for the view of the River from here is open from Hammersmith to Kew Bridges, a significant part of the course rowed by the Oxford and Cambridge boats. These houses have not only old-established gardens at the back, but also front gardens with moorings, at the water-side of the roadway along the Mall, a feature that adds to the charm of this geographical survival from an age that has almost vanished.

Hammersmith Mall has not withstood the assault of the nineteenth and twentieth centuries so well. But it has kept Doves Building, and Kelmscott House, both of historical interest for people who love good book-production. Cobden-Sanderson had his printing-press at The Doves, where he designed books in much better taste both in format and typography, than those from the much more famous Kelmscott Press run by William Morris, whose book-design was frequently so black-letterish in its medievalism that the text was almost unreadable. The first format of *Everyman's Library* produced in 1906, showed how the influence of the Kelmscott Press persisted into the present century. Morris had his printing press in a cottage in Upper Hammersmith Mall, near Kelmscott House where he lived for the last eighteen years of his boisterous life.

A. P. Herbert, amateur lighterman, versatile author, and for many years Parliamentary representative for Parnassus in the House of Commons, is a veteran inhabitant of Hammersmith Mall.

[5]

Having strayed again from my course, I may as well beat about the southern suburbs, thus following nostalgic memories of childhood rather than the chart into which, at the start, I proposed to reduce the overwhelming abundance of London. Had I followed my whim more freely, I should have gone straight from Brixton to Herne Hill. Or I could have approached my private little holy ground by leaving Kennington for Camberwell Green, along the A20 main road for Kent, turning right at the Green up Denmark Hill. At a corner site, like the prow of a ship, once stood a

*Huguenot Cemetery,
Dulwich Village.*

suburban music hall, the Camberwell Empire, now one of the *Lost Empires*, about which Mr J. B. Priestley writes in his novel (of that title). Little Tich, T. E. Dunville, Marie Lloyd and Daisy Dormer, performed there again and again, worshipped by the habitués, but disapproved by the large puritan element which dominated the suburbs at that time. All are vanished now, the stage, the stars, and the louring zealotry of the sectarians.

The road that turned off to the right by the Camberwell Empire was called Cold-harbour Lane. There are Coldharbour Lanes in many English towns, and towns called Cold Harbor in several of the United States. The name caught my imagination when I was a boy, and often I walked on up the Hill, forgetful of my rather dreary sur-roundings at that stage of my return home from Camberwell Green, as I pictured the possibilities of what a cold-harbour might be.

Further up the Hill, a bifurcation to the left enclosed a wedge-shaped piece of grass-land and trees that was a plague-pit into which the bodies of victims of the Great Plague of London in 1665 were tumbled. The close around the Green is called Champion Hill, and the top of it was until recently a leafy lane that wound down the eastern side of the Hill to Dulwich Village, past the grounds of one of the big houses posed in a majestic colony of wealth over the summit of Denmark Hill. Bessemer, the Victorian inventor of hardened steel, built an observatory in his grounds. For long after his departure, the creeper-clad dome survived as a landmark to be seen from the approach to Dulwich Village. There it slept on a summer day, still foreign above the green slope of the almost rural hillside, indicative of mental adventure beyond reason, to the mind

Buskers. (Overleaf).

of a youth just awaking to the lure of the lonely science of astral mathematics, beyond the range even of the God of his orthodox childhood, hitherto so comforting.

Until the disrupting changes accelerated by the two world wars, Dulwich Village remained as a rural community only four miles from Charing Cross. Denmark Hill and Herne Hill made a kind of Andes Range to cut it off from London and the inner suburbs of Brixton and Camberwell. Peckham and New Cross were hidden by the lower reaches of the vast range of the Sydenham Heights. Thus the Village was a Shangri La, remote, safe from eventuality, changeless within its green monastery of trees. That was how a boy saw it.

The uniqueness of the neighbourhood began at the summit of Denmark Hill, which overlooks the paradisal valley in which Dulwich nestles. At this spot, the man ultimately responsible for this astonishing preservation is said to have knelt and thanked God that at last his long quest was rewarded.

Edward Alleyn was an actor-manager who made a fortune in the theatre on the South Bank of Southwark. Shakespear and Marlowe were contemporaries, and he took women's parts in their plays. His second wife was the daughter of the Dean of St Paul's Cathedral, John Donne, who in that capacity tried to forget that he had been a poet of passionate intensity whose technique opened a new vein in English prosody, not to be fully explored until three hundred years later.

Alleyn also worked with Richard Burbage (the first actor to undertake the part of Hamlet) and Philip Henslowe, a more mundane participant in theatre-life, as well as being a money-lender and a brothel-landlord, two of the more remunerative professions in our all-too-human society.

The stage was in such low esteem in the sixteenth and seventeenth centuries that to associate it with those other two enterprises was not thought to be incongruous. Alleyn's reputation was not smirched by his business association with Henslowe. Nor was his character. He was a good and pious man, and the determination later in his life to devote part of his fortune to the foundation of an almshouse for old folk, and a school for boys, was quite in keeping with that character.

Alleyn paid £5,000 for the Manor of Dulwich in 1606 from the estate of Sir Francis Calton, a goldsmith who had acquired it in settlement of a debt from Henry VIII. The King held it as part of the vast lands of the Abbey of Bermondsey, which came to the Crown at the time of England's first great capital levy.

Alleyn's purchase included the house called Hall Place, and here he lived for the rest of his life, which came to an end in 1626. During that time he built the Old College which stands today at the southern end of Dulwich Village, considerably altered during the intervening centuries. It was damaged during the 1940–45 war, and in the course of the repairs the Italianate arcade at the back was removed, together with the decorated leaden water tank, which gave a foreign charm to the wholly English garden behind the College.

196

Alleyn named his college 'of God's Gift', an act of piety which harmonized with the provision in his will that trees on the Dulwich estate should be preserved. Thus the village has kept its rural character, with a High Street shaded by elms and chestnut trees, standing in greensward strips that accompany the street through the village, past the Old College, the Picture Gallery, the gates of Dulwich Park, and up College Road as far as the public school, which stands in its playing fields, an Italianate intrusion, heavily ornamented, built in 1866, to accommodate sons of the increasingly wealthy middle-class, during a process of education never envisaged by Alleyn.

The Old College buildings form three sides of a quadrangle, open toward the Village. The central range is shaded by a cloister, behind which the chapel stands under a wedge-shaped tower. The interior of the chapel is dark, with heavy woodwork, and the organ is notable because the black and white keys of the manual are reversed. Handel once 'touched those tender stops', commanding a congregation many of whose members probably had never been over the hill to London. When I was a boy at the village school called Dulwich Hamlet, from 1905 to 1908, several of my classmates were similarly untravelled.

The Art Gallery was the first public gallery in London. The building, which stands behind the Old College, is a demure example of the work of that stylist John Soane. It was built in 1811. The entrance was formerly from Gallery Road, which forks to the righthand of the College from the High Street. It gave into a poky lobby. War damage put an end to that inconvenience. The restored Gallery is now approached from College Road, opposite the Park Gates, and entered through a spacious vestibule more worthy of the rest of the building and its contents.

Fortunately, the restoration has not increased the size of the Gallery, which can display only a part of the property at one time. That property includes the nucleus left to the College by Alleyn. His own portrait, and a self-portrait by Richard Burbage, are of historical value as contemporary records, but of little worth as works of art.

Various gifts to the Gallery were made during the passage of time, but as late as the middle of the eighteenth century Horace Walpole wrote off Dulwich Gallery as containing 'a hundred mouldy portraits among apostles, sybils and Kings of England'. At the end of the century, an art dealer named Desenfans found himself landed with a valuable collection of pictures which he had been buying for the King of Poland. But Poland suffered one of its periodic partitions and the king was deposed. Desenfans offered the collection to the British Government, to found a National Gallery. The offer was refused, and Desenfans left the pictures to his friend Bourgeois, a Fellow of the Royal Academy, who in turn left them to Dulwich College, together with £12,000. This munificent gift established the Gallery at that time as the most important in the country.

The widow of Desenfans gave another £4,000 to the College, and the architect John Soane was commissioned to add a west wing to the College to house the pictures, and a mausoleum to contain the coffins of Mr and Mrs Desenfans and their friend Bourgeois. We can stare through a pink glass pane today, at these relics of a lasting benevolence.

Smaller gifts have since been made, amongst them a set of five superb portraits by Gainsborough of members of the musical Linley family. The donor was a Linley who held the post of organist to the College from 1816 to 1831, years that must have passed as gently over the rural village as did those when I was a schoolboy there, enraptured by my translation to this paradise from the sinister marshes of Battersea.

I haunted that Gallery, when I was free from school; and being of a disposition affected by poor health, I revelled in the solitude of its rooms. In those days there seemed to be no public interest in the arts. Picture galleries were trysting places for lovers seeking an assured solitude. My inclination toward drawing and painting was fostered by a gifted and sympathetic art mistress at Dulwich Hamlet School, and I spent my Saturdays either studying the masterpieces inside the Gallery, or drawing in the garden behind it, my only companions the single custodian inside, and the gardener outside, both old wiseacres who shook their heads sadly over a boy given to such inactive pursuits.

The arrangement of the pictures at that time was in the Victorian convention. They hung from waistline to ceiling, covering every inch of the walls. Only a half of them could be seen in detail, or to aesthetic advantage. Teniers, father and son, were lavishly represented there, and their art gave me a perspective line for my lifelong interest in landscape painters. I learned to believe that Rubens is the greatest of them all, and that the genius of Gainsborough eclipsed the talent of Joshua Reynolds. One picture, 'Jacob's Ladder' by Rembrandt, filled me with awe. It had made a similar impression, nearly a century earlier, on another boy, Robert Browning, who was born in 1812 in Peckham, near the present Camberwell School of Art. He too, as I did, wandered about in the Dulwich Woods above College Road, wearing childhood's garment of imagined invisibility, a poet-prince in an uninhabited universe, with reality hidden over the next hill.

In his first published poem, 'Pauline', written when he was eighteen, Browning cried

> Up for the glowing day—leave the old woods;
> See, they part, like a ruined arch, the sky!
> Nothing but sky appears, so close the root
> And grass of the hill-top level with the air—
> Blue sunny air, where a great cloud floats, laden
> With light . . .

Those woods were Dulwich Woods, five miles from Charing Cross.

The shabby, provincial interior of the Gallery has vanished since the reconstruction after war-damage. Today, Soane's gift of style, of exquisite taste, has been cleared of all the clobber that hid it. The pictures are hung, each to advantage, in rooms furnished with Persian rugs and antique cabinets and tables. I do not exaggerate in comparing the Gallery today with the Ryksmuseum in Amsterdam.

How beautiful still is the environment round the College and Gallery. Look at Bell House, almost opposite the new entrance gate to the Gallery, and backing on to the Park. It is like a chapter from a Jane Austen novel, in terms of architecture and garden lore. Further up College Road, and looking across it to a grove of giant trees called Lovers' Walk, is a little house half hidden behind high hedges, that might have sheltered Mrs Gaskell while she wrote *Cranford*. In fact, or rather in fiction, Dickens made Mr Pickwick retire there after the convivially benevolent adventures that brought fame to his author at the age of twenty-four.

Later the Irish novelist George Moore discovered the secretive beauty of Dulwich, and pictured it in his book *The Lake*. There is now a Dulwich Society, which works devotedly to preserve and maintain the mystery of this little oasis set in the desert created by the internal combustion engine, and the aesthetic nihilism engendered by it in human society.

Even so, the greasy tide of twentieth century mechanism is creeping through the Village. The toll-gate in College Road is a pathetic barrier against it, but is likely soon to be swept away, so that the High Street can become an unimpeded track for motor traffic to and from London. No historical relic, no architectural or natural beauty, no sensibility or function of the individual, can resist for long the rage of this Gadarene fever of speed, whose symptoms appear in every aspect of the way of life of mankind.

[6]

College Road rises to the top of Sydenham Hill, and the long esplanade that formerly lay in front of the Crystal Palace. Below the esplanade crouched the railway station, terminus of the line that carried visitors from Town to the Palace. The traffic was spasmodic, according with the programme of events taking place in the Palace or its grounds.

Paxton's futurist pleasure-dome, designed for the Great Exhibition of 1851, could not have been more happily placed than on the top of Sydenham Hill, its second and last home after the Exhibition in Hyde Park was closed. It became a picturesque landmark from Kent and Surrey, its exotic structure accepted as part of the familiar scenery of the outer London heights, just as we accept the turban of the oriental gentleman peddling cotton goods round our English streets and countryside.

Croydon, the new face of London. (Overleaf).

199

Something was always happening at the Crystal Palace during its perpetual commission, until the night it was destroyed by fire in 1936. The full-sized theatre at the west end of it was used by travelling companies offering such plays as *The Royal Divorce, Magda, Caste, Bluebell in Fairyland*. It was a strange experience to visit the theatre on a night when the rest of the Crystal Palace was out of action. My brother and I discovered that by going an hour too early, we could wander about under the vast roof, to stare up at the giant organ in the central dome famous for grand-scale performances of the 'Messiah', with Santley and Clara Butt as soloists. We could lose ourselves amongst the hundreds of classical statues, reproductions in plaster-of-Paris, that by this proxy brought to Sydenham 'the glory that was Greece, and the grandeur that was Rome'. We could seek out in the lower, and smelly regions, the zoo of wild animals. We could stare, through eyes glaucous with boredom, at exhibits from Orient and Empire, now mouldering away after their great purpose in Hyde Park in 1851, and their subsequent retirement to Sydenham.

All this freedom was that of visitors to a desert and uninhabited island. If by chance we saw a human being, it would be a dusty, dispirited maintenance man, probably also left over from the Exhibition, all hope abandoned now. When at last we entered the theatre, the half empty auditorium, its histrionic plush faded to mole-colour, seemed by comparison with the Palace that contained it, a bower of gaiety and abandonment.

On the night when the Crystal Palace was burned down, I felt my childhood going up in smoke; all the rich improbabilities, the magnificent incognitos, the sense of secret royalty and fabulous habitations. Now, I thought, the rest of life is down to earth. I could have wept. But being adult, hardened by experience, I did not. Instead, I went down to the oyster-bar in Chancery Lane, and fortified myself against dejection, with a dozen and a glass of draught Guinness. Even so, I could see in the plate-glass mirror behind the barman, threatening the gold lettering, a flickering of flames.

Today, a television mast stands on the site of the Crystal Palace. Great schemes are in hand for making a national sports stadium in the grounds that slope away on the Surrey side of Sydenham Hill down to Penge, the strangely remote suburb where the poet Walter De la Mare lived for many years. London has engulfed that retreat, and spread out to consume Beckenham, West Wickham, Addington, Shortlands and Bromley, all sylvan villages half a century ago, each with its distinct community and pride of place. Yet, by the miraculous intervention of Edward Alleyn's will, drafted three and a half centuries ago, Dulwich survives, though it lies under the London side of the hill. The village street has changed but little. The Georgian Beech House, sideways on to the road, and creeper-clad, has been displaced by a row of villas. But the Huguenot cemetery, with its wrought-iron gateway, and its tombs reminiscent of Gray's 'Elegy', is still there, sinking deeper every summer beneath its pall of green.

[7]

Trying to recollect where I have strayed from my itinerary, I stand once more against the balustrade on Crystal Palace Parade, and look northward over London. It is a clear day, and in the distance I can see the further rim of the saucer, the heights of Hampstead and Highgate, the latter instantly recognizable by the spire of the parish church on its summit. That must be about ten miles away.

Central London, the London of the ages, scarred with history, lies in front of me, under a blue sky. Below the blue hovers a thin veil, too fragile to obscure my view of the main features. In places, over the power-stations of Battersea, the World's End, Bermondsey, the veil thickens, but still not enough to hide the pattern, or absence of pattern, of the streets and buildings below. There the huge fabric lies, a carpet of green near at hand, picked out with a tracery of roofs. But brick and slate soon predominate, and my mind becomes irritated by the effort to differentiate, and name, the thickening clusters of houses, gardens, chimney-stacks, streets and railways running away into the middle distance, where whole parishes dissolve into the confusion.

Formerly it was more possible to place this town hall, that church spire, the gleam of the canal penetrating from the Surrey Docks as far south as the Walworth Road. But so much has changed, so much has been replaced by uniform blocks of tall ferro-concrete, that our old Londoner is at a loss to recognize the features of his home town.

Far eastward, looking along the onetime nondescript stretch of semi-slums between the Tower Bridge and Greenwich, the city-scape is laid with high groups of flats like a board with chessmen. Crawling round the bases of them, the patched-up terraces that housed the pre-war folk of Bermondsey and Greenwich in squalor can still be seen.

As the panorama gathers toward the centre, individual features become both more recognizable and more unreal, for the thin veil of smoke, a condition of the air rather than an actuality, obscures the foundations of the great riverside monuments, and sets them floating in space. Thus I see St Paul's Cathedral buoyant on a dream; and there is the Tower Bridge, or rather its upper half. To the left of the dome of St Paul's I can distinguish the smaller one of Old Bailey; and more clearly, the Shell-Mex tower on the site of the Hotel Cecil, and the white Savoy Hotel next to it, all shapes as un-anchored as a procession of cumulus clouds. I have the illusion that they are moving up river; but I see that it is the visible atmosphere which is deceptive, not they.

From this viewpoint, the new buildings can be seen for what they are; signatures of the latter half of the twentieth century, self-contained and conceived out of no co-operation between their architects, yet shaped by the spirit of the age, a new-world character, the bully of Mother Nature, subservient only to the genius of mathematics, the demon who is already coaxing us to rear for the stars, as it once coaxed Icarus.

As I stand here, an old man alongside the ghost of his boyhood self, both leaning with their midriffs squashed against the balustrade of Crystal Palace Parade, I recall the line from Wordsworth's sonnet which I quoted at the beginning of this book.

'And all that mighty heart is lying still.'

It puts me to shame for my gloomy thoughts as I stare into the future symbolized by the forest of ferro-concrete which begins to dominate the prospect of London, with an almost mortuary significance.

For that 'mighty heart' is not lying still. During every lull in the traffic behind me along the Parade, I can hear a faint sound. At first I thought it was the pounding of the blood in my ancient veins, after my effort to achieve the impossible, a coherent journey that should encompass the whole of London.

But the sound has no such individual source. It is in the air. It fills the whole of that great plain lying between me and the heights of Hampstead and Highgate. It escapes into the open haze to east and west.

I look at the invisible figure beside me, myself of sixty years ago, and know that he too is listening; for the sound is filling now not only space, but also time. It goes on: it has been going on, with a gradual increase through the centuries, for two thousand years.

It is the sound of that 'mighty heart' beating, with a relentless health, thrusting the life-blood of London through the great arteries, into and out of the side streets, the alleys, the homes, theatres, churches, dens and brothels; every individual of its eight million souls a microcosm contributing to that increasing vitality, with the accessory instrumentation of wheels, pistons, slamming doors, gushing taps, and every other moving object in contact with another object; the scream of women in labour, the whispering of lovers in delight, the shouting on Exchange, the din of self-intoxicated adolescents in the coffee-bars and jazz-clubs, the debating in Parliament, the praying in church and chapel, and the thud of earth on the coffin, after the farewell, the tears, the remorse.

This is the perpetual orchestration of humanity, day and night; before, during and after every change, every triumph, every disaster. It is the voice of power, that absolute power which roars through the veins of a leaf, and in the explosion of a star. It never ceases. It goes on, the maker and consumer of circumstance. It has created, and continues to create mankind, and through this cunning instrument it weaves civilizations, whose nodal points are cities.

London is among the greatest of them. It is almost a macrocosm of the history of man. It generates and contains something of everything human. Nobody can write about it without realizing this, and being driven almost to despair by the paradox. That devoted honorary Londoner Samuel Johnson, in his poem on London written in 1738, when he was a young man newly settled there and expectant of taking it by storm, wrote

> Here malice, rapine, accident, conspire,
> And now a rabble rages, now a fire;
> Their ambush here relentless ruffians lay,
> And here the fell attorney prowls for prey,

and later in the over-long poem, the bitter disappointment of his naïve hopes of instant triumph in London vents itself as

> This mournful truth is everywhere confessed,
> Slow rises worth, by poverty depressed:
> But here more slow, where all are slaves to gold,

204

Where looks are merchandise, and smiles are sold;
Where won by bribes, by flatteries implored,
The groom retails the favours of his lord.

But thirty years later, when dining with Boswell at the Mitre, he said, 'The happiness of London is not to be conceived but by those who have been in it'.

All is true, both what Johnson said in youth and in age; and so is the contradiction. Like life itself, London can only be approached subjectively, and therefore piecemeal according to the dimensions of our consciousness. London is thus both infinite and eternal, so long at least as human beings exist.

There is every reason to fear that we are on the brink of annihilation, like that overweening Icarus. But this mysterious power whose pulse I can detect as I stand on Crystal Palace Parade, with my coadjutor self by my side, is that life-force, that love, which 'casteth out fear', and by its own urge demonstrates a faith that over-rides reason. Hiroshima, Rotterdam, Plymouth, Dresden, were almost completely destroyed during the last war. But they are still there, gradually to build up a *persona* related to their past, and amplified by the disaster that has changed their physical manifest.

London has suffered too, during this twentieth century of Armageddon. Before the century ends, and the fit of racial insanity subsides, London may have worse to follow. But even if it shares the fate of Hiroshima, it will arise out of its own ashes, as enigmatic as ever, gradually to accumulate its innumerable contradictions, through which it has been recognized in the past, and will be in the future, by its awe-stricken historians, its architects, its painters and its poets.

Down below the Crystal Palace.

INDEX

Names of persons, places and monuments in roman type; selected topics in *italic type*; illustrations in **bold type**.